D1156804

Tradition and Authority

Key Concepts in Political Science

GENERAL EDITOR: Leonard Schapiro

EXECUTIVE EDITOR: Peter Calvert

Other titles in the same series include:

Tradition and Authority

Carl J. Friedrich

WITHDRAWN
IOWA STATE UNIVERSITY
LIBRARY

Praeger Publishers

New York · Washington · London

Published in the United States of America in 1972
by Praeger Publishers, Inc.
111 Fourth Avenue, New York, N.Y. 10003, U.S.A.
5 Cromwell Place, London, S.W.7, England

All rights reserved
Library of Congress Catalog Card Number: 74-95674

No part of this publication may be reproduced, stored in a
retrieval system or transmitted in any form or by any means,
electronic, mechanical, photocopying, recording or otherwise,
without the prior permission of the Copyright owner

Printed in Great Britain

JC571
F695
c.1

Contents

924536

924536

'Key Concepts'
an Introductory Note

Political concepts are part of our daily speech—we abuse 'bureaucracy' and praise 'democracy', welcome or recoil from 'revolution'. Emotive words such as 'equality', 'dictatorship', 'élite' or even 'power' can often, by the very passions which they raise, obscure a proper understanding of the sense in which they are, or should be, or should not be, or have been used. Confucius regarded the 'rectification of names' as the first task of government. 'If names are not correct, language will not be in accordance with the truth of things', and this in time would lead to the end of justice, to anarchy and to war. One could with some truth point out that the attempts hitherto by governments to enforce their own quaint meanings on words have not been conspicuous for their success in the advancement of justice. 'Rectification of names' there must certainly be: but most of us would prefer such rectification to take place in the free debate of the university, in the competitive arena of the pages of the book or journal.

Analysis of commonly used political terms, their reassessment or their 'rectification', is, of course, normal activity in the political science departments of our universities. The idea of this series was indeed born in the course of discussion between a few university teachers of political science, of whom Professor S. E. Finer of Manchester University was one. It occurred to us that a series of short books, discussing the 'Key Concepts' in political science would serve two purposes. In universities these books could provide the kind of brief political texts which might be of assistance to students in gaining a fuller understanding of the terms which they were constantly using. But we also hoped that outside the universities there exists a reading public which has the time, the curiosity and the inclination to pause to reflect on some of those words and ideas which are so often taken for granted. Perhaps even 'that insidious and crafty animal', as Adam Smith described the politican and statesman, will occasionally derive some pleasure or even profit from that more leisurely analysis which academic study can afford, and which a busy life in the practice of politics often denies.

It has been very far from the minds of those who have been concerned in planning and bringing into being the 'Key Concepts' series to try and impose (as if that were possible!) any uniform pattern on the authors who have contributed, or will contribute, to it. I, for one, hope that each author will, in his own individual manner, seek and find the best way of helping us to a fuller understanding of the concept which he has chosen to analyse. But whatever form the individual exposition may take, there are, I believe, three aspects of illumination which we can confidently expect from each volume in this series. First, we can look for some examination of the history of the concept, and of its evolution against a changing social and political background. I believe, as many do who are concerned with the study of political science, that it is primarily in history that the explanation must be sought for many of the perplexing problems of political analysis and judgement which beset us today. Second, there is the semantic aspect. To look in depth at a 'key concept' necessarily entails a study of the name which attached itself to it; of the different ways in which, and the different purposes for which, the name was used; of the way in which in the course of history the same name was applied to several concepts, or several names were applied to one and the same concept; and, indeed, of the changes which the same concept, or what appears to be the same concept, has undergone in the course of time. This analysis will usually require a searching examination of the relevant literature in order to assess the present stage of scholarship in each particular field. And thirdly, I hope that the reader of each volume in this series will be able to decide for himself what the proper and valid use should be of a familiar term in politics, and will gain, as it were, from each volume a sharper and better-tempered tool of political analysis.

There are many today who would disagree with Bismarck's view that politics can never be an exact science. I express no opinion on this much debated question. But all of us who are students of politics—and our numbers both inside and outside the universities continue to grow—will be the better for knowing what precisely we mean when we use a common political term.

London School of Economics
and Political Science

Leonard Schapiro
General Editor

To the memory of my friend
Alexander Rüstow
who knew about true authority

Part I
Tradition

1/Tradition as Fact and Norm

Tradition and authority are so closely linked in writings on political theory and philosophy that it is very difficult to discuss one without taking up the other. Max Weber made tradition one of the sources and hence one of the types of authority and of legitimacy as well, contrasting it with charismatic and rational-legal sources.[1] In doing so, he remained in the well-known habit of the Enlightenment which contrasted reason and authority. The implication was that the methods of reason were scientific as contrasted with the methods of authority based upon revelation or irrational belief. And much of that belief had its base in tradition. The possibility that both tradition and authority might themselves be rational was more or less excluded for thinkers of this 'tradition'. Charles S. Pierce wrote a generation ago that 'when the method of authority prevailed, the truth meant little more than the Catholic faith'.[2] This is a typical statement, although incorrect in itself. For the method of authority also implied tradition, as exemplified in the writing of Edmund Burke (see below). Such uncritical rationalism is based upon the assumption that 'the method of authority' is some kind of unreasonable superstition which must be superseded by 'scientific method'—an argument which provided the basis for Auguste Comte's philosophy of history. I do not propose to pursue this line of argument further at this point for I shall return to it later on. Even what has been said shows that anti-traditionalism and anti-authoritarianism are closely linked. It is my intention in this study to show that neither authority nor tradition is unrelated to reason and reasoning, and more particularly that tradition is often the very basis of reasoning and rational argument. Aristotle in his *Rhetorics* makes this point very clear, and the 'New Rhetorics' of our times has done the same.[3]

Tradition, then, is here understood to possess a vital function in the body politic. It provides the basis of much communication and effective integrative argument. This function has caused tradition in the normative perspective to have been frequently under- or overestimated. It has been underestimated in revolutionary periods, and overestimated in post-revolutionary and static periods. The fact of the matter is that tradition varies in its importance for the political process, both in time and for different groups. When Goethe wrote the famous lines, 'What from your forebearers you inherited, earn it in order to possess it truly!' he was concerned primarily with the value of tradition for the individual, but our concern in these pages will be the function of it in the community, including the individual. There is little question in modern social science that an individual cannot be conceived of outside of tradition. Individuality develops in a person's accepting certain features of the values and beliefs traditional to the society into which he is born, while rejecting others. Likewise craftsmen, artists and scholars (as well as scientists!) learn a traditional craft, art or field of learning and then are able to contribute to it by altering it in some particular respect. Politics is no exception. The drama of the challenger of tradition in Wagner's opera *Die Meistersinger* is a drama familiar in political life. Its rich suggestiveness may be seen in showing how tradition may hinder and hurt as well as help and support a given craft, although Wagner, the romantic revolutionary and friend of Bakunin, sympathizes with the innovator and gives insufficient credit to the function of the Beckmessers who uphold tradition. To be sure, too much tradition ossifies a political order, but equally surely too little tradition undermines and dissolves the community and its order.

The word tradition derives from the Latin *tradere* which means to transfer or to deliver. The term has a religious or ecclesiastical root, as does so much of our political vocabulary. The very words of the founder and leader must be transferred and delivered from generation to generation. A great historian of the Christian religion has written that tradition is 'the delivering of a precious deposit, whose source is held to be divine, to a specially selected person'.[4] The Confucians, perhaps the most traditionalist, if such a comparison be permitted, made the transmission of the words of the Master the focal point of their effort. Theirs was a political vision. They achieved an extraordinarily stable order. Eventually, it exemplified the danger of such stability, of such strong tradition: the empire became stratified to such an extent that it collapsed like a house of cards when confronted with foreign challenge, but one may well ask whether it was only the super-structure that did. Mao's frantic effort to exterminate the Confucian tradition by the so-called 'cultural revolution' proved the persistence of Confucianism, and it suggested that the last word has not perhaps been spoken in this matter. Another case illustrating the powerful impact of tradition is that of Israel. After the dispersion (AD 70) the Jewish culture has persisted nearly two thousand years without any governmental structure of the people as a whole; it has been preserved within the framework of a priestly and communal order.

In a highly significant recent study it has been shown that charisma and tradition are not necessarily contradictory: Gandhi's leadership was based upon traditional roots and culminated in a radical transformation of a tradition which still informs much of Indian politics. The analysis is built upon the contrast of tradition and modernity and upon the assumption, rightly, that 'they infiltrate and transform each other'. The authors are objecting to the assumption of the enthusiasts of modernity with its stress upon 'rationality' that tradition is useless and valueless, and who would therefore relegate tradition 'to the historical trash heap'. Such notions derive, of course, from the assumption that 'modernity will be realized when tradition has been destroyed and superseded'.[5] I agree with this analysis when it asserts that 'the assumption that modernity and tradition are radically contradictory rests on a misdiagnosis of tradition as it is found in traditional societies', as well as upon a parallel misunderstanding of modernity, and of rationality. If adequate attention is given to what Weber liked to call *Wertrationalität*, that is to say, a rationality based upon values, a better understanding not only of rationality and hence modernity results, but also tradition is understood as rational and as capable of absorbing rationality. In Western Europe today, the tradition of constitutionalism is the tradition of *Rechtsstaat*, of government according to law, and law in this connection means reason and rationality. It may mean the artificial reason of the law which Edward Coke spoke of when he characterized it as 'that which has been refined and perfected by all the wisest men in former succession of ages, and proved and approved by continual experience'.[6] Such a traditionalist view of the law which claims at the same time to be a rational one is in sharp conflict with certain natural law doctrines,[7] such as those expounded by Francis Bacon. The issue is so central to our topic that it may be permissible to cite Coke once more in a passage which specifically addresses itself to the problem of law and reason. Coke wrote in his *Reports* that:

> Reason is the life of the law, nay the common law itself is nothing else but reason; which is to be understood as an artificial perfection of reason, gotten by long study, observation and experience, and not as every man's natural reason . . . by many succession of ages the law of England has been fined and refined by an infinite number of grave and learned men, and by long experience grown to such perfection, for the government of this realm, as the old rule may be justly verified of it, that no man out of his private reason to be wiser than the law, which is the perfection of reason.[8]

Clearly this is a declaration of war against the scientific temper personified by Francis Bacon, and the scientist could not admit that his findings were the result of 'private' reason; for science is neither private nor public; it searches for laws of nature that are eternal and unalterable. The dialectic tension between tradition and rationality (modernity) may be expressed in the paradox that there can be no discovery of reason in nature except by the traditions of scientific inquiry, and these traditions of scientific inquiry are in their way a 'perfection of reason' just as much as Coke claimed for the law.

The issue is one related to that circumscribed by the triad of reason, rationality, and religion.[9] There is a similarity to be observed in the process of arguing from precedent in the common law and in the theological discourse; to these in turn is related the kind of arguing from ideology which prevails in contemporary autocracies. In all three cases, the politically key question is who possesses the authority to say what is true, that is, what is 'tradition' or what is law or what is the meaning of the ideology. Reasoning from tradition is a key method of authority, and the attacks on authority are usually especially directed against such reasoning from tradition. Sacred texts, such as Magna Carta, the American constitution, or Karl Marx's *Capital*, not to mention the Bible, are cited as embodiments of tradition, and hence prove what is right, in conduct or communication. The fact that words are never certain in their meanings, and the less so the more abstract the referent to which they are meant to refer, while often deplored therefore offers a considerable range of discretion to him who has the authority to answer such questions as, What does Confucius say? By this means tradition becomes pliable. To cite our historian once more: 'In face of traditions become obsolete an appeal was made to other traditions, or to the Bible; where written testimony was uncertain or awanting [sic], recourse was had to tradition; that is, that was declared to be tradition which was not to be justified under another title.'[10]

Such authoritative interpretation occurs in all kinds of contexts, and serves the vital function of integration of the political community. For it incorporates into tradition innovative elements which eventually transform the tradition into something quite different. Such change may, in fact, as observed before, become itself a tradition, even if hedged in by such phrases as 'peaceful change', 'evolution rather than revolution', or 'constructive criticism'. Even so, political tradition poses real problems for effective political change. Certain behavior patterns resist rapid change. Much of what goes under the name of 'national character' and is misunderstood by thinking of the behaving individuals, actually constitutes political tradition and may be radically altered by a change in the political environment. The old tale about German Communists when arriving at Unter den Linden in their march upon the center of Berlin dutifully dividing their column so as not to violate the prohibition against stepping on the lawn in the middle of the street is only one among many illustrations. But while this is true enough, it is equally true that such behavior does change when the environment changes. The twentieth-century Englishman does not closely resemble his countryman in the seventeenth and neither the latter's enthusiasm for long-winded argument, nor the modern Englishman's easy-going ways, were shared by his countryman of another age. A political tradition, we may define in the light of these and related facts, is more specifically a set of convictions and beliefs concerning political community, including the behavior of men as political persons. Political tradition defines how rule is conducted, and how the ruled behave towards their rulers, including their electing and controlling them. To turn the definition around, such tradition is embodied in habits, customs, and norms which express the prevalent values and beliefs.[11] To avoid the nominalist fallacy, one might also say that it is an established fact of political experience that prevalent values and beliefs are expressed in the habits, customs, and norms of a political community, and it is proposed to designate these as its tradition. Hence what is meant by tradition is its consensus, or its *concordia* as earlier writers said.[12]

It is clear from what has just been said that tradition or consensus need not mean an agreement on fundamentals as has often been asserted, unless the behavior of political persons is seen as a fundamental. But to be 'fundamentally at one', as Lord Balfour once put it, is rarely found, and was surely a euphemism as applied to Victorian and post-Victorian England. A measure of consensus exists in any political order, but no discernible optimum can be identified. Tradition seen as a set of established values and beliefs having persisted over several generations is, therefore, the antithesis of ideology with which it is often confused by those who see any system of ideas as an ideology.[13] But a programmatic set of ideas concerned with the change and/or maintenance of a political system which an ideology properly speaking is, contrasts sharply with tradition as here defined. Traditionalism, on the other hand, may become an ideology. As a self-conscious and deliberate insistence upon the value of tradition, making it a norm of behavior, it is, of course, itself an ideology or may become one when it is elaborated into an action program, and the cast of such an ideology would be reactionary. Therefore traditionalism needs to be clearly distinguished.

Nationality and nationalism cannot be described except in terms of a national tradition, although writings on these subjects rarely concern themselves with the questions which this term raises. German authors have been fond of speaking of a common *Geschichts-erlebnis*, a shared historical experience, and the image of national heroes no doubt shapes the behavior of individuals in a nation. Great poems, such as *Iliad* and the *Song of Roland*, exercise a continuing influence. As they are learned by the young, they become part of a national tradition in the above defined sense. Of course, the nation is not the only kind of political grouping to which this applies, parties, local units, and other kinds of formations in modern pluralistic societies elicit intense loyalties in similar terms of a group tradition. Fraternities and clubs, as well as military formations cultivate traditions in the hope of developing loyalty and an *esprit de corps*. All this goes to show that the role of tradition is ubiquitous and related to the very basis of politics. It may be doubted whether politics is possible, except perhaps in short periods of revolutionary upheaval and of the ardor of a founding process, without a considerable amount of tradition. It is one of the most striking features of such innovative situations how quickly the revolutionary impulse is transformed into traditional ways, how quickly ideology becomes doctrine and the accompanying behavior becomes ritual.[14]

It has become the fashion to speak of the processes of transmission of a political community's verbal and behavioral stock as 'socialization'. Such socialization has been defined as 'the process of induction into the political culture'.[15] What is involved here is a learning process in the course of which the young discover what it takes to become a political person in a particular cultural setting. The term socialization is therefore misleading, and education (traditional term!) or the French *formation* is much to be preferred. For it stresses adequately that these processes are not only 'socializing' but 'personalizing' and 'humanizing' as well. The uneducated infant becomes a human being as it absorbs, adopts, and adapts to the ways of its elders. It is not true that a human person exists apart from the society into which he is born and is then 'socialized'. Tradition not only socializes him, but it personalizes him, as Rousseau so well understood and depicted in his *Emile*.[16] When the French speak of *formation*, they rightly stress that a being is being formed, that is, moulded and cast into a particular form. This process is based upon tradition—upon a complex of values, convictions, beliefs, habits, customs, and super-stitions—which changes, but slowly. Rousseau called it the true constitution and remarked that political philosophers had given little attention to it. 'It is not graven on tablets of marble or brass, but on the hearts of the citizens.' Rousseau was very insistent about its not being static. For it 'takes on every day new powers when other laws decay or die out, restores or takes their place, keeps a whole people in the ways in which it was meant to go, and insensibly replaces authority by the force of habit'.[17] We shall return to this passage in the next chapter for its historical signi-ficance. Here it is important to note that Rousseau clearly insists upon the vital function of tradition for the political community, as well as on its steady evolution. The education of citizens[18] consists in inculcating this tradition, not as a static and unalterable doctrine, but as a meaningfully evolving set of beliefs as to what is right.

The Greeks had a word for it, and it was *nomos*, the hallowed ways of the ancestors, like the Chinese *li*. Plato's basic concern was to find a viable alternative to its religious base. For the religious source of *nomos* having disintegrated, and a state of *anomie*[19] having resulted, that is, there being no longer any sacred custom and hence no basic law to guide men's actions, a rational basis had to be found. We shall in the next chapter adumbrate the resulting problems. Here we merely note that in a sense Plato's thought revolved around the problems of tradition and the pos-sible alternatives to tradition as integrators of political community.

In defining tradition in analytical, functional terms, it is impor-tant not to allow it to become a fetish. Nothing is good just because it has existed a long time, just as nothing is bad because it has done so. Traditionalism insists upon a presumption in favor of what has endured, but the opposite assumption may have greater validity. The American soldiers who defended their sacrilege of blowing out an eternal flame in an Oriental temple by observing that it had burned long enough voiced the protest of the young against the old in a crude and dramatic way. One may properly doubt that they had reflected upon the claim to truth which the particular revelation had that the eternal flame symbolized. Tradition as such is a formal concept which may become associated with any content, true or false, beneficial or noxious. Traditionalism is therefore rightly seen as a pejorative term, since it is a species of obscurantism.

In contemporary political science, it has become customary to employ the term in such a sense. The writings of past political thinkers are spoken of as the tradition, and scholars writing in this tradition are spoken of as 'traditionalist'.[20] It is an 'un-modern' way of dealing with political phenomena, whereas the 'modern' way is the truly scientific way, that is to say, the 'quantitative' and the 'behavioral' way. Again tradition is being confronted with modernity as if the two excluded each other. However, a careful scrutiny of the results of such 'modern' studies discloses that they are full of tradition, as they ought to be, and that the position they take is quite 'traditional'. The results in terms of problem-solving are not often very striking which suggests that the methods adopted are not well-adapted to the materials in hand. You cannot split wood with a hammer, nor drive a nail with a sledge. All science is the result of an interweaving of tradition and of challenges to tradition. New departures presuppose a thorough mastery of the traditional way. Much of it may be 'tacit knowledge', as Michael Polanyi has called it, but it is knowledge just the same. Hence all good science and scholarship is always based on tradition, as is all craftsmanship. It is too often forgotten that sciences are crafts, as are arts, and little good work can be done if artisanship is gainsaid. The bane of the social sciences especially is the untraditional handling of the conceptual framework which mistakes a change in terms for genuine discovery and new insights.

What is true of the science of politics and government is equally true of their practice. In democratic politics especially, the lure of rhetoric is great, and a new vocabulary is taken or rather mistaken for genuine innovation. The 'new freedom', the 'new deal', the 'great society', 'the social free market economy', the 'new democracy', and so forth—these are slogans which exaggerate the degree of innovation actually involved. They turned out to be old wine in new bottles, and at times even old wine in old bottles. When French and German politicians try to co-operate in the building of an integrated Europe, many of their problems are the result of national traditions, and they may manifest themselves in seemingly small matters such as the handling of documents and the conduct of discussions. The neglect of such detail has caused basic troubles, such as those which arose in the conduct of parliamentary government on the continent of Europe when a rationalist parliamentary procedure such as that which Bentham had worked out[21] was adopted instead of the traditional procedure associated with parliamentary government in Great Britain.[22] The main shortcomings of Bentham's scheme resulted not so much from its general conception, rationalist and utilitarian, as from the neglect of features of the real situation. I have shown elsewhere that to consider the making of laws the main business of parliamentary assemblies was disfunctional when actually the fighting of the government by criticism was more important.[23] The behavior of representatives in their assemblies in Britain, France, and Germany, expressive of deep-rooted national traditions, needed to be taken into account. The failure to 'play the game' and to do it according to fair play, often commented upon, offers a striking illustration of these difficulties. Manners are a key to politics; for without manners, the game deteriorates into fighting according to the 'law of the jungle', 'where anything goes', and 'chaos becomes king'.[24]

2/Traditionalist Theory

Tradition has, as a concept, played an important role in the history of political thought only in modern times. But since tradition is a basic aspect of politics, the phenomenon and its possible normative value have been recognized since Plato, at least. The stress which Plato laid upon the importance of *nomos* is essentially traditionalist, if traditionalism is taken to mean an outlook in which the normative value of that which has been 'in the time of our forefathers' is stressed and maybe even glorified. For Plato the question was central. In his autobiographical *Seventh Letter* he describes how deeply he was disturbed by the disintegration of the old order and how he came to see it as his task to reconstruct the political order by providing a rational, that is to say, a philosophical foundation for a *nomos* which no longer could rest upon traditional notions of goodness and of right conduct: *nomos*. Pindar's famous line about *nomos*, that he is the father of all things (*nomos pater panton*), makes it even more apparent that *nomos* very clearly suggested to the Greek mind what tradition does to us: the sacred transmitted beliefs, rituals, thoughts of our ancestors. What concerned Plato was the inclination of recent generations to make *nomos* relative: these very norms which were meant to have absolute binding force. The sophistic outlook of a Callicles, in its extreme cynicism, was, Plato felt, the logical outcome of sophistic questioning of sacred tradition. The concept of *nomos* itself had undergone a basic change: 'The original concept of *nomos* as a proud order of universal obligation had become, under the influence of rationalist thinking which spread far and wide by the middle of the fifth century BC, the prevailing but usually erroneous opinion of the many.'[1] It was a process similar to what has happened to tradition; once a sacred transmitted truth, it is now seen as a staid and misleading prejudice. The flavor of

'Fourth-of-July oratory' illustrates the point. What was once the unchallengeable truth of 'self-evident' propositions has become the empty rhetoric of vulgar speeches.

Plato's hope of replacing the certainty of sacred tradition by the certainty of metaphysical insight (*sophia*) in lieu of opinion (*doxa*) was doomed. Aristotle realized that at least in a free society, the opinion of the many had to be taken seriously and could not be discarded in favour of the ideas of an intellectual élite. It was still possible to revive tradition, he believed, if adequate attention were given to the task of rhetoric. In exploring the potentiality of rhetoric,[2] Aristotle fully recognized the importance of arguing from past tradition, including *nomos*. Tradition had acquired a function, to use modern parlance, namely that of 'integrating' the political community.

It was not very far from here to the Stoic version of Pindar's doctrine that 'the *nomos* is the ruler of all divine and human things'.[3] If *nomos* is here taken to mean 'sacred tradition' it demonstrates how far thought had advanced attaching a very high value to tradition, how definitely thought had come to see tradition in normative terms. It has been asserted that when the Romans submitted their own thought to the inherited tradition of Greece, they made thereby the Greek heritage a tradition in the specific sense. Tradition became a conscious taking-over of what was another's, and before this striking adoption of an alien heritage tradition in its specific sense was unknown.[4] If one disregards the highly traditionalist history of Oriental thought, such a statement is perhaps true, though I believe as I have shown that Plato and Aristotle, and hence their followers, had a distinct notion of tradition. It was the Romans, however, who demonstrated a deep sense of tradition, as particularly manifest in their law and its history, as contrasted with the Greek philosophers who derived a revolutionary doctrine from their grasp of the implications of the loss of tradition (*nomos*) which had occurred. The manner in which the ancient law of the Tables was preserved through many generations of skilful interpreters[5] is not only a monument to human ingenuity, but also to the power of tradition, not to be repeated until the coming of Common Law. The same might be said of the adroitness with which Augustus managed to preserve the political traditions of the Republic in the rituals of decision-making by Senate and popular assemblies. Such an operation presupposed a highly sophisticated appreciation of the political function of tradition as a preserver of political order which finds a parallel in British and American constitutional practice. Those latter-day sceptics who came to discourse upon the constitution as a 'political myth' are greater adversaries of that tradition than its opponents—the rebels who at least took the tradition seriously.

The Romans had, after the Middle Ages in which tradition was seen in the faith of the Church, their true disciple in Machiavelli and the Renaissance for which he spoke. Machiavelli knew that tradition is a powerful *motif* in shaping political conduct. He warns the princes to respect the beliefs of his subjects, that is to say, their traditional convictions, and points out how deep and bitter will be the reactions of men whose traditions are not respected. The true revolutionary will, of course, want to destroy such traditions, and Mao's cultural revolution was an imposing attempt to uproot a great tradition which had begun to re-assert itself against the revolutionary regime of his making. The deeply traditionalist Confucian tradition which many an old China hand had expected to block Communism was to be destroyed by a book-burning more vast and ruthless than others had attempted before him, including the great Emperor Shi Huang Ti.[6] Machiavelli was convinced, following Polybius, that religion was the basis of a soundly constructed state, and this political and functional view of religion, derived from the Romans, rested upon the view that religion embodies the moral traditions of a people.[7] It was a view later popular with Rousseau and others who talked of a 'civil religion'. That such notions are deeply traditionalist should be obvious; for it is the capacity of religion (*religio* derives from the words that mean 'to bind'!) to create firm bonds that recommends it to the builders of states. Actually, tradition often elicits religious fervor in its adherents, and its violation then appears as sacrilege. Machiavelli puts it rather simply: 'And as the observance of the ordinances of religion is the cause of the greatness of a state, so their neglect is the occasion of its decline.'[8] This thought is taken from Polybius who had assigned to the piety of Romans a major share in explaining the city's greatness. Religion provides the bond, that is, for the maintenance of the tradition of the ancestors, and the Senate was called upon to watch over its observance as its authority (*auctoritas*) had to reinforce the decisions of the people (see below Chapter 10). It has not been sufficiently recognized that Machiavelli revived this traditionalism of a strictly political sort; it was his substitute for the traditions of the Christian faith which had moulded thought and action in the Middle Ages.

Secular traditions became vital in the period of the English revolution, and it was Sir Edward Coke and others who founded the traditionalism which has been so characteristic a feature of British politics. Burke eloquently restated it in the later days of the French revolution, and against its rationalism. Nor were Sir Edward and his partisans newcomers in the field. They built upon and expanded what had already become a firm conviction of Britishers, through the work of Sir John Fortescue, Sir Thomas Smith, and Richard Hooker. The constitutionalism which was at the core of this tradition was seen as distinctive and indeed as unique, even though it bore a marked resemblance to medieval constitutionalism on the continent. The sharp contrast to the royal predominance in France—its 'absolutism'—made of this constitutionalism a tradition of all-pervading vitality. Hooker and Sir Thomas Smith formulated the philosophical implications of England's particular political order. This basic order, constitutional and hence legal, was seen as resting upon the people's assent. All other laws derive their obligation from it. It is the tradition of the Common Law which Sir Edward Coke pitched against the tradition of the natural law, derived from the Middle Ages and theologically defended by King James and Sir Francis Bacon.[9]

We cannot here explore the complex argumentation which developed over this dialectic, but Coke's statement of the tradition as contrasted with the reason or rationality of the natural law must be cited for it represents a major step in the crystallization of traditionalism as a conscious doctrine. 'Life, or Inheritance, or Goods, or Fortunes of his [the King's] Subjects are not to be decided by natural Reason, but by the artificial Reason and Judgment of Law, which requires long study and experience . . .'[10] In the introduction to his famous *Institutes* Coke had warned against any rash change in the law, calling it 'most dangerous'. He there stated his conviction that 'that which has been refined and perfected by all the wisest men in former succession of ages, and proved and approved by continual experience cannot but with great hazard be altered and changed'. It is the doctrine of the 'artificial reason of the law'.[11] It constituted an important ingredient of traditionalism: its legal basis. Whereas in ancient China (and indeed elsewhere) the innovative and antitraditionalist notion of man-made legislation of the 'legalists' had been pitted against the traditionalism of classical learning, here the tradition of the law is made the norm superseding the revolutionary potential of royal sovereignty and of the prerogative[12] which triumphed on the continent and more especially in France.

The revenge came upon the monarchy in the revolution. The anti-traditional absolute sovereignty was now vindicated by rationalists in the name of the people who were determined to eradicate tradition root and branch. In the discussions prior to the revolution, and more particularly in the work of Montesquieu, the voice of tradition had already been heard. Some of the arguments against royal absolutism were cast in terms of an older order, namely medieval, feudal constitutionalism. Montesquieu's analysis of what he called 'the spirit of the laws' already amounted to a thorough stress on tradition; for what is the spirit of the laws? What moulds a people's laws? Its tradition, its customs, habits, and beliefs. In the usual analysis of Montesquieu's stress upon the individuality of nations and their ways it has often been overlooked that tradition is being stressed as the prime factor in shaping national destinies. That view is also echoed in Rousseau's doctrine of the 'true constitution' discussed above (see Chapter 1).

At this point, the resemblance between Rousseau, presumably the progenitor of the French revolution, and Edmund Burke, its most persuasive adversary, suggests itself. George Sabiné has stressed it, but in terms of community. He interpreted the two great political theorists as 'rediscoverers of community'. They were rediscoverers of tradition as well, and the close relation between tradition and political community as its essential bond explains it. But Burke was much more explicitly concerned about tradition. His technical terms are different, but the key to his argument is that tradition is a better guide in politics than is ratiocination. It has rightly been said that Burke's ideas on prudence as a political virtue, on the nature of society and government, on the importance of manners and religion, are all interrelated with his defence of tradition.[13] Burke's traditionalism evidently had deep personal roots. He once said 'I feel an insuperable reluctance in giving my hand to destroy any established institution of government, upon a theory, however plausible it may be.'

Burke, in discussing tradition, employed mostly the term 'prescription'—a legal term derived from English property law. Prescription refers to a common law doctrine according to which immemorial use and enjoyment of a thing constitute a valid claim of title to it. When applied to the political order, it amounts to an assertion of the value of tradition. Burke saw the constitution as 'an elaborate fabric fitted to unite private and public liberty with public force, with order, with peace, with justice, and above all, with the institutions formed by bestowing permanence and stability, through the ages, upon this invaluable whole'. Hence 'it is the result of the thought of many minds, in many ages. It is no simple, no superficial thing . . .'.[14] The many flowing phrases in which Burke celebrated the British constitution as virtually a divine creation all breathe the reverence for tradition. Society, Burke thought, is 'a partnership'—a partnership that is in all science, art, and every virtue and all perfection. It is a partnership of the living, the dead, and those yet to be born. Linked with custom and convention, with heritage and the wisdom of one's ancestors, tradition is a guide superior to all rational theory. The English revolution was made, he liked to recall 'to preserve our ancient, indisputable laws and liberties, and that ancient constitution of government which is our only security for law and liberty'. And he mentions the Petition of Right of 1628 which claimed that 'your subjects have *inherited* this freedom', and which spoke of 'rights of Englishmen' and not of 'rights of men', 'a patrimony derived from their forefathers'. Arguing against

the men who sympathized with the French revolutionaries, Burke
thinks that Englishmen 'preferred this positive, recorded, *heredi-
tary* title' to a vague speculative title. 'This new and hitherto
unheard-of bill of rights . . . belongs to those gentlemen and their
faction only—namely the revolutionaries.' For that reason, Burke
would draw a sharp distinction between change and reform. To
reform is to preserve by necessary change, whereas to change is to
destroy the very nature of an institution. At one point, in his
Letter to a Noble Lord who had criticized him for getting a pension,
he stressed that 'it was not my love, but my hatred of innovation,
that produced my plan of reform'. And in his *Speech on the Plan
for Economical Reform* (1780) he asserted that it was 'a plan which
should have both an early and a temperate operation'. This was
the spirit which inspired his *Speeches on Conciliation with America*.
'We must all obey the great Law of change. It is the most powerful
law of Nature, and the means perhaps of its conservation. All we
can do, and that human wisdom can do, is to provide that change
shall proceed by *insensible degrees*.' (my italics).

Such stress on gradualness is an important feature of English
traditionalism. To the argument from law is here added the argument from nature and history. As such it blossomed forth into the
imposing structure of Hegel's philosophy of history—perhaps the
most elaborate argument on behalf of tradition which has been
produced by Western thought. Tradition is not necessarily a
romantic concept, but it became a mainstay of romantic thinking
about politics when the Burkean enthusiasm for the British ways
was made the basis of a similar enthusiasm for such remote and
hence inaccessible political orders as the medieval one. Such sentiments mingled with a widespread reaction against the French
revolution and Napoleon's conquests and violence and produced a
number of explicitly traditionalist writings, notably in France,
where not only the monarchy but also the Catholic Church were
providing a focal point for such thought. It belongs to the age of
restoration. Misnamed, because the *ancien régime* was not and
could not be restored, the political order was none the less struc-
tured on the *tradition* of the *ancien régime* as much as possible.[15]
Hence the traditionalism of its three ideological apologists: de

Maistre, Bonald, and Lammenais. All three followed the lead of Burke, but applied it to the old order of royal France.

Joseph de Maistre, the most significant of the French traditionalists, at least for our purpose, actually spoke of Burke as 'the admirable Burke'.[16] Yet, he followed him only in part. For the centre of de Maistre's thought is occupied by the tradition of the Church; in his work *Du Pape* he even advanced a carefully reasoned argument for papal infallibility. (This issue will be taken up later in connection with the discussion of authority. See below Chapter 4.) In connection with the restoration of the monarchy, de Maistre advanced a proposition which became a *locus classicus*, a 'word with wings' as the Germans say. 'The re-establishment of the monarchy which is called counter-revolution, is not going to be a counter-revolution, but the contrary of a revolution.' When one returns to tradition, it is not a revolution, but the return to sanity and truth. But de Maistre was not only concerned with the concrete events after 1789; for him the revolution is an 'epoch', namely the Age of Enlightenment. What de Maistre combats is the thought of this epoch, and more especially that of Voltaire. Voltaire is the great antagonist whom he wishes to exterminate, to excise from the mind and thought of France. That he failed is obvious enough; for France lives to this day in the thought of the revolution. It itself has become *the* mainstream of tradition of French civilization.

De Maistre tries to resuscitate the ancient constitution of medieval France. He sharply rejects the view of those who maintain that France did not have a constitution by pointing out that a constitution need not be written; the notion that only written law is truly law he combats as an outgrowth of that belief in reason which is the source of all trouble and which he decries. 'Qu'est-ce que cette lumière tremblotante que nous appelons *Raison*?' (What is this flickering light which we call Reason?) He speaks of reason with mocking contempt, and because of the feeble guidance which reason can offer 'no nation can give itself a government'.[17] For each nation lives by its tradition of immemorial origin and 'each nation, like each individual, has a mission which it must fulfill'. This notion, so extensively elaborated by Hegel in his philosophy of history, is the key to much traditionalism; for through it tradition becomes a key value. In the case of France, de Maistre adds that she 'exercises over Europe the function of a veritable judge-ment [*magistrature*] which cannot be contested, but which she has abused in a most culpable manner'. France was at the head of Christianity, and it is not for nothing that her king was called *très-chrétien*. But now she has used her influence to demoralize Europe, and is being punished for it.[18] This line of reasoning suggests that a tradition is not only an inspiration, but also a burden of responsibility: to fulfil one's mission. Biblical notions, including that of the chosen people, inject themselves into such a conception of tradition. It is sacred and he who would defend it must eradicate thought destructive of its core. De Maistre, who called eighteenth-century rationalism 'philosophisme', saw philo-sophy as a 'puissance délétère', a deleterious force which is pre-occupied with destruction.[19] He looks upon the eighteenth century as terrible and destructive of the great monarchical tradition of France. His is a truly reactionary conception of tradition and is linked to the overestimation of duration and stability. The spirit of the Enlightenment, by contrast 'denies all, shakes all, protests against all'. These accusations are actually hurled at Locke who brazen-facedly says No, to everything. His philosophy is the pre-face to eighteenth-century philosophy; it is all negative and there-fore null and void. The beginning of all wisdom is to despise Locke.[20]

De Maistre loved paradox which is part of the distinguished style by which he excels all other traditionalists. He had a deep sense of language as the core of tradition. The community of language seems to him a visible manifestation of national unity. His philosophy of language has many points in common with that of the Romantics. 'The fraternity which results from a common language is a mysterious bond of immense force,' he wrote.[21] In the next chapter something more will be said about the linguistic aspect of tradition and traditionalism. Here it needs to be stressed that de Maistre in the tradition of the *esprit de finesse* argues against the *raison raisonnante* in terms of experience. The *petits faits significatifs* which William James would one day stress in his prag-matic struggle against abstract rationalism and idealism are by de

Maistre united in the *grand fait significatif*: GOD. De Maistre's traditionalism wants to be realistic. This realism is carried to the penultimate point in de Maistre's infamous apotheosis of the hangman: 'All grandeur, all power, all subordination depend upon the executioner: he is the horror and thereby the bond of human society. Remove from the world this incomprehensible agent: that very moment order is replaced by chaos, thrones fall and society disappears.'[22] In such a declamation, traditionalism betrays its reactionary core. It is not, as in the case of Montesquieu, a force for ameliorating society, but the drawing of a veil over brutal force in defense of material interests and of established power. Montesquieu had mobilized tradition for liberty and progress. Only a balance of established powers can secure liberty; for in obeying the laws men are free. Hence Burke could praise Montesquieu as the greatest political genius of the eighteenth century; he recognized in him the traditionalist who sought to combine stability with change through a balanced constitution.[23]

If space permitted, it would be worthwhile to explore the related thought of other French traditionalists who were contemporaries of de Maistre, such as Mon-losier, Bonald, and Lammenais.[24] But such a sketch would not add significantly to what the brief analysis of de Maistre has shown, namely that the most innovative dimension which they added was the religious one of the Christian faith. Thus the circle is closed, and what *traditio* meant in the beginning, namely the transmission of sacred revealed truth, also stands at the end of the long history of political thought on tradition: its truth is not argued, but revealed, it is not proven, but believed. As Bonald put it at the end of his analysis of political and religious power: 'Happiness—you do not find it but in religion, in virtue; and the virtue of a people is only its justice.'[25] Beyond lay the modern vistas of a tradition grounded in a more or less rational ideology—the 'isms' of the nineteenth and twentieth centuries to which some pages will be devoted in the next chapter.

3/Tradition and the Science of Politics

In the twentieth century tradition has become a pejorative term. To say that someone is a traditionalist means to call him an old dodo, a man out of tune with the modern, the scientific, the progressive trends. This is curious; for the great Russian revolution and its aftermath, the Stalinist terror regime, would seem to call for the same kind of traditionalist reaction which occurred in Europe after the French revolution. To be sure, there were flickerings, such as the American Liberty League which embodied a reaction to the New Deal. Also, the politics of the German Federal Republic has been spoken of as a restoration. There are markedly traditionalist features to the post-Second World War constitution-making, a process I have called 'negative revolution', since the Hitler regime had already pre-empted the title of counter-revolution.[1] The Fascists generally talked a good deal about tradition, and more especially 'the grandeur that was Rome'. But the more striking developments are in the fields of political science and sociology. One notes with surprise that the *International Encyclopedia of the Social Sciences* has no entry under this heading, but other related subjects are amply treated. It is a curious fact that, perhaps in reaction against the normative implications of the traditional term 'tradition', other words have been employed to discuss the phenomena formerly treated under this heading. There is ideology, and political culture, and national character—all these are fashionable terms which occupy the foreground of social scientists in recent years.[2] It remains to discuss them in this perspective, though at best our observations must remain sketchy in view of the range of issues involved.

It was Karl Marx (and Friedrich Engels) who first spoke of the superstructure of ideas in a given society as ideology and meant by it the society's tradition. It is perhaps due to that fact that Max

Weber in his magisterial treatment of authority and legitimacy, as already noted above (see Chapter 1) spoke of tradition as one of the three possible sources of authority and legitimacy. But in doing so, he did not discuss tradition, but rather treated it as a matter of course. The same easy-going propensity we find in Eisenstadt's recent comprehensive *Political Sociology* wherein a number of key sections contain the reference to 'traditional' regimes or societies, without any careful analysis of what is to be understood by tradition except that it is not 'modern' and that it is not 'rational'. We have tried to show in the first chapter how dubious that particular confrontation in fact is. In any case, by reading between the lines, one discovers that Max Weber 'defines' tradition in passing as 'that which has always existed' (*das immer gewesene*) when discussing the attribution of legitimacy,[3] and he elaborated this passing remark when discussing types of legitimate rule. Here he says that legitimacy may be of a 'traditional character', that is, it may be based upon 'the everyday belief of the sacredness of prevalent traditions'. This is an obvious *petitio principii*. Weber further asserts that the primary types of traditional rule are those which lack a personal administrative staff of the ruler; he speaks of gerontocracy (rule of the old), and primary patriarchalism. In the elaboration of these assertions, the term 'tradition' is used often, but without further indicating what is to be understood by it, and mainly by contrasting it with rational and charismatic forms. We cannot here enter into the elaboration, let alone the many 'cases' which Weber adduces to illustrate his notions. What matters for us is that Max Weber made tradition a major category in the analysis of political phenomena—he added the sociological dimension, as had Comte done before him; the conception of tradition becomes a category of sociological analysis, even though taken unrefined and in the common understanding.

It is more than doubtful that many political orders or systems of rule were ever based upon a belief that they had *always* existed. In fact the foundation myths which play such a vital role in political tradition as such contradict the Weberian concept of tradition.[4] Indeed, a tradition need not even have existed a long time. Its original meaning of something that has been transmitted (*traditum*) suggests its location in time. This dimension is particularly evident in the case of ideology. The text of Marx may be sacred to the rulers of the Soviet Union, and transmitted to them by authorized persons, but Marx is a historical personality, and constitutes a subject of research and controversy. Yet, there exists now a definite Soviet tradition of interpreting Marx and Engels (as well as Lenin) which is transmitted from generation to generation in home, school, and university, as well as through the means of mass communication, and it is no longer possible to understand or even to describe the Soviet Union without recognizing this as a basic fact of Soviet life.[5] But ideological tradition is by no means limited to the Soviet Union or to Communist regimes. Perhaps the most striking case of ideological tradition is that of the United States. Grounded in such highly ideological documents as the Declaration of Independence and the Constitution, the political tradition of the United States seemed until recently almost impregnable. By being an ideology of progress toward an unattainable goal, this tradition was subject to a particular dialectic, as is that of the Soviet Union, for it was a self-transforming tradition: what the tradition required was that men acted differently from the way they had traditionally acted. In a sense it was a revolutionary tradition, and maybe it still is or will prove to remain so. 'Fourth-of-July oratory' has traditionally been afflicted with this inner contradiction. At the moment, in the preparation for celebrating the bicentenary of the Declaration, the official body quickly faced the challenge that it is not in the tradition of the American people to look backward. Therefore a suitable celebration would not face toward 1776, but toward 2076. It would ask: what should a constitution be like which would be suitable and effective for the next hundred years?[6]

In a very interesting study on what the American 'common man' believes, Robert E. Lane was able to show, on the basis of extensive interviews in a small Connecticut town, that Americans of varied backgrounds continue to be attached to the ideology which constitutes the American tradition.[7] To be sure, the government has taken the place of God in some respects as the rectifier of what is wrong in their environment as Americans see it. Lane's approach to the problem of tradition is typical of contemporary political science: to inquire into the data of politics, rather than to speculate upon them as Burke and de Maistre had done. Did Englishmen really believe what Burke alleged? Did Frenchmen really think what de Maistre claimed to be their thoughts? We do not know, and hence are inclined to accept the brilliant assertions of these writers. Do Americans really follow the tradition which they express to a skilled interviewer? Lane himself does not know; he expresses some doubt from time to time, by adding 'at least they say so'. But in any case, the tradition appears in the garb of an ideology.[8]

This contemporary approach to political science also found a new concept, denominated as 'political culture', or 'civic culture'. Derived from anthropology, the term culture is here taken to mean the congeries of behavioral traits that are associated with politics, that is to say, its tradition. The authors who have given the term wide currency[9] define it as follows: 'The civic culture is not a modern culture, but one that combines modernity with tradition.' Without further ado about what is to be understood by tradition, the authors proceed to illustrate their points by the example of Great Britain. 'The development of the civic culture in Britain may be understood as the product of a series of encounters between modernization and traditionalism . . .'[10], culture by them being taken to mean 'psychological orientation toward social objects' and the political culture of a nation as 'the particular distribution of patterns of orientation toward political objects among the members . . .'[11] In contrast to Britain, 'in France, Germany, and Italy the encounters between modernizing tendencies and the traditional powers seem to have been too massive and too uncompromising to permit the emergence of a shared culture of political accommodation'.[12] It seems fairly clear from these passages that tradition is here taken to mean that which is present when a wave of 'modernization' hits a particular political order. Modernization appears to be an abstraction standing for 'democracy' and industrialization. That this conflict could also be described as the clash between two traditions is evident. For modernity is largely the political tradition of Britain and America. The terms employed introduce evaluations: the Anglo–American tradition is better or good compared with that of France, etc. The authors make no attempt to argue such a preference; it is taken for granted. What matters to us here is that the argument as such is cast in terms of traditions. That an alien tradition may be transmitted and may transform a native tradition is an insight which stands at the beginning of reflection on tradition, as we have seen in the Roman case.

In order to penetrate and perhaps transcend the obscurity in which such a discussion shrouds the problem of tradition, the category of national character has recommended itself to the modern mind. It is a category of popular parlance which is widely and indiscriminately used in the literature on nations and has only recently become the subject of scholarly inquiry and discriminating analysis.[13] The approach to national character has often been attempted in terms of the individuals concerned, and then led to assertions about the typical Frenchman, German, or Englishman. Leaving aside the often propagandistic intention of such discussions,[14] such an approach is subject to the methodological difficulties of typology. The classical method for discovering the 'typical' in a class of things or events is to compare them to discover what is alike and what not, and then to construct the average type. The typical American or Frenchman is thus a human being who, while resembling in many traits other human beings, is characterized by a few traits which are found in greater frequency among Americans and Frenchmen than among others. A typical American is gregarious, a typical Frenchman polite, so it is claimed. Whether such national types can be scientifically demonstrated to exist may be an open question; they are certainly believed to do so.[15] Hence the controversial notion of a 'national character'. Throughout the epoch of nationalism, that is, since the French revolution, culture was taken as something God-given, something that always was there. Having accepted a given set of cultural traditions writers then proceeded to explore their effects without much regard for the possibility of changing these cultural traditions themselves. Much of the writing on national character was and is based on this kind of argument. What was to be proved was taken for granted. How a national tradition came to be what it is was explained by its being a manifestation of the national character. And what is a national character? A national tradition or culture.

At this point, it becomes clear that the question of national character may be seen as a collective rather than an individual phenomenon, that a national character need not be manifest primarily in the traits of individuals, but in the traits of a culture. Such traits of a culture, shaped by the nation's history and the cultural creations to which it has given rise, may be readily identifiable through great documents, such as the Magna Carta, Dante's *Divine Comedy* or Goethe's *Faust*. But such identification, although the core of a national tradition for many, usually is not certain, but leaves room for much doubt and controversy. Thus the 'meaning' of the Declaration of Independence has changed over the years, and even today is far from unequivocal. Each nation, and every other group, will restate its self-understanding from time to time. But such restatement will always be built around traditional features; it may challenge the tradition, but it is likely to do so in traditional terms. Revolutionaries may want to change all, but they find that in acting, they act in the ways of a nation's or group's tradition. When the German Communist revolutionaries avoided stepping on the lawn on Unter den Linden they manifested this truth in a comical way. When General Clay, on taking leave of his command in Germany in 1949 addressed the Germans, he expressed to them his confidence that they would succeed in setting up a viable democracy. Of course, he said, it will be different from American democracy 'but their constitution happily combines German democratic traditions with the concept of representative government and a rule of law which the world has come to recognize as requisite to the life of a free people'.[16] It is a clear case of transmission of a tradition, the American democratic tradition, but it is also a clear case of how such *traditio* affects and alters what is transmitted. I commented on this problem in discussing the political order after 1949, by pointing out that 'after all is said and done, German notions of democracy and government have continued to play a predominant role in shaping this result',— namely the Basic Law of 1949.[17]

Lloyd and Suzanne Rudolph have, in connection with a study of the role of tradition in India[18] developed a very challenging position on the complex interrelationship of tradition and modernity. Besides giving an interesting characterization of modernity in contrast to tradition, they have (rightly) insisted on their inter-relationship and denied that they are dichotomic, that is to say, absolute alternatives. 'The assumption that modernity and tradition are radically contradictory rests on a misdiagnosis of tradition as it is found in traditional societies, a misunderstanding of modernity as it is found in modern societies, and a misapprehension of the relationship between them.'[19] This relationship, far from being dichotomic, is in their view 'dialectic'. Whatever that may mean, the important point is that a tradition contains inherent contradictions which may become procreative of change. This point we have stressed above in reference to certain traditions of the modern West, such as the American and the scientific one. They show that it is equally true of the Indian tradition. In a masterly analysis of Gandhi's work, they demonstrate how he turned elements of the Indian tradition to use in producing a vital and viable change in India.[20] In short, the modernization of India may proceed and is proceeding in an Indian way, as the demo-cratization of Germany did in a German way. It all goes to show that tradition need not be interpreted in juxtaposition to modern-ization and modernity. Rightly they warn that 'there is of course nothing natural or inevitable about modernisation that connects congenial elements of the old society to the needs of the new. Nothing may happen; tradition and modernity may not connect'.[21] There is involved here the factor of creativity with its unpredictable ways. Thought, as well as action, is involved. Not only consti-tutions and the like are relevant to political tradition, but modes of thinking.

Hannah Arendt, in her discussion referred to above stresses tradition in philosophy. She argues that a great tradition going back to Plato and Aristotle (why not Socrates?) had come to an end in the nineteenth century, that Marx, Kierkegaard, and Nietzsche had destroyed this great tradition and thereby inaugur-ated the age of totalitarianism. 'Our tradition of political thought had its definite beginning in the teachings of Plato and Aristotle. I believe it came to a no less definite end in the theories of Karl Marx.'[22] And she adds that 'Marx' own attitude to the tradition of political thought was one of conscious rebellion'.[23] True enough, but it does not prove that the tradition against which he rebelled therefore came to an end. If it 'would have been a contradiction in terms to realize philosophy or to change the world in accordance with philosophy', as Arendt alleges, she must presume that Plato's model republic was by him considered unrealizable, which is manifestly not true. Not only in the *Laws*, but in the *Statesman* and the *Republic* the city which is laid up in heaven is definitely thought of as a potential reality, and Plato's trip to the tyrant of Syracuse proves how dead serious he was in his will to change the world.[24] It may therefore be seriously doubted whether the philosophical tradition Arendt talks about either had such a beginning or is now at an end.

Contemporary development suggests, indeed, its continuing vigor. A contemporary philosopher of science, C. F. von Weizsaecker, has suggested that tradition has a continuing role to play in philosophy, not the particular tradition Arendt discussed but tradition in general.[25] He starts with the assertion that 'man has to have tradition', and he cites as support the phenomenon of language. The steady progress of mankind is unthinkable without language. But which language a man learns is not fixed. He learns it from his parents, he learns it from his companions and his social environment, and he thus adopts the tradition which is embodied in this language. Man could not be what he is without a tradition through which he learns a language and thereby not only words, but modes of behaviour, customs, and insights. The will to preserve these has been counterbalanced by the will to change, to progress. Traditionalism and progressivism are thus embedded in the very essence of human existence. Even in science, progress is conditioned by tradition, you cannot make a significant contribution without knowing the past achievements. This argument is persuasive in the case of the natural sciences where tradition is understood as the preservation of past progress. The situation is less clear in the social sciences, but is actually equally true. The contemporary faddists of new methods who speak with contempt of the old hands as 'traditionalists' are unaware of the violation of basic scientific tradition. But a sense of this persists: when two researchers recently queried large numbers of the behavioral school of political scientists they discovered to their amazement that the highest degree of agreement among these was on the importance of studying the classics.[26] Weizsaecker tells how he searched to find the foundations of modern science and eventually found himself back with Kant. Kant, however, proved difficult to understand, and so he proceeded to Descartes and from him to scholastic philosophy and to the Greeks. 'Thus it was my experience,' he said, 'that I was not able to understand the quantum theory, and until now I cannot understand the quantum theory without understanding Plato.' And to understand him one must grasp the questioning of Socrates. He then illustrates this from Socrates' speech, before the court which condemned him, in which he describes his search for wisdom and his finding that he did not know. 'Thus he is the real father of philosophy,' concludes Weizsaecker. We agree. And this great tradition which knows that tradition is only partially right, that it must be subjected to questioning in the hope of progressing to a better one is in politics the tradition of the 'open society', the tradition which recognizes the value, but also the limits of tradition! Tradition in this perspective is not a sure guide, but a tentative guide, and the ideological tradition is the more reliable, the less it is dogmatic and hence fanatic.

Tradition, then, political tradition poses, as mentioned, very serious problems for effective political change. It has often been remarked that even the most violent revolutionary thrust fails politically to alter highly relevant folkways. Reflections upon this persistence of tradition help to explain why traditionalism appears in certain political constellations. Traditionalism is a philosophy which belongs with a time following upon revolution, or a time of crisis preceding such a revolution. Crisis and revolution challenge established values and beliefs, and an explicit reaffirmation of them is the response of those who accept the existing order of things. Hence Arendt's argument is inherently misleading; the challenge of Karl Marx served to stimulate a reaffirmation of traditional philosophical positions, though not those which Arendt mistakenly stated them to be. Max Weber's great work is such a reaffirmation; it is in its entirety an effort to overcome the Marxian challenge of a 'materialist' interpretation of history.[27] There were other responses which were more specifically political, such as the reformulation of classical libertarian and democratic political theory, in quite a number of works.[28] It is also true of the Christian tradition with the reaffirmation of which Catholic and Protestant writers have been occupied.[29] Beyond these lies the tradition of the university. Crucial for all three, the liberal, the Protestant, and the Catholic, and vital to the functioning of the political order through its dedication to the search for truth, those who are committed to it, and to the extent that they are, will of necessity withdraw from the battle cries of the market place into the quiet of laboratory and library, there to examine the assumptions upon which the actions of rulers and their helpers are based.[30]

Part II
Authority and Reason

4/The Rational Ground of Authority

To recall what was said at the outset, ever since the eighteenth-century revolt, freedom-loving intellectuals and their following have viewed authority with hostility. They have denounced it as the source of much, if not all, evil. The anarchists have taken a satanic view of it. In the spiritual sphere, authority was linked to the Christian faith and its ecclesiastical shepherds, in the secular to royal absolutism and later to capitalist enterprise. There always was and is an implication that authority relates to unreasoning superstition, to some thinly veiled despotism and exploitation. And it was and is argued that 'the method of authority' must be superseded by the clear voice of reason. Rational discourse and scientific inquiry must take the place of this method of authority. Rarely was it recalled that rational argument and scientific conclusions depend upon authority. Nor did the revolutionaries realize that their claim to assent and obedience was a highly authoritative one.[1]

In reacting to such a line of thought, conservatives have, since Bonald and de Maistre,[2] glorified authority beyond all reason. The sharp-witted attacks by de Maistre upon eighteenth-century rationalism and more especially upon its most renowned spokesman, Voltaire, revolve around the issue of authority against reason. Because reason, *raisonnement*, had led to the dissolution of all social order, to terror and anarchy, men ought to and are in fact ready to subject themselves to authority unquestioningly. Contemporary conservatism often argues the same line. Order is made the battle-cry of those who would demand the submission to authority, no matter how irrational. Thus, authoritarians and anti-authoritarians agree in radically juxtaposing reason and authority, in insisting upon a juxtaposition, an unbridgeable dichotomy between these basic features of human behavior. But are reasoning and authority so antithetical? Does authority have no basis in reason? Does reason ever prevail without an element of authority? The following analysis seeks to show that authority and reason are closely linked, and indeed it develops the proposition that much authority rests upon the ability to issue communications which are capable of reasoned elaboration, and that authority which does not so rest is feeble and short-lived. The prevailing and erroneous view is often linked to a confusion of authority with power, or even based upon treating the two as synonymous, that is to say, 'the same thing'. (Much anarchist writing is vitiated by this error.) It can almost be said to be common usage. In more learned discussions, authority has at times been defined as a particular kind of power, as 'formal' power or as 'rightful power'.[3] Authority has been claimed for persons, but also for things, such as a dictionary or the law. The problem of what makes people accept authority, obey a command or believe a statement has given rise to a variety of interpretations of authority. In such connections, authority has been contrasted with freedom or with force. It has been praised and condemned in all these juxtapositions. As a result, authority has been made the basis of a pejorative adjective, authoritarian. Authoritarian regimes have been personified in authoritarian personalities, and such an authoritarian personality has become the incorporation of the devil. Much of the writing in this field seems to suggest that this is not only an objectionable, but an eradicable trait. And as a person must cease being 'an authoritarian', so society must be rid of structures and institutions which call for such personalities. The battle of German university reformists to eliminate the *Ordinarienuniversität*, the university dominated by full professors, highlights this struggle against authority. Rarely was it recognized that the argument really was one for replacing one authority, namely that of the professors, by another, namely that of the students and assistants. Authoritarian personalities have of course turned up among these groups as readily as among the professors.

In most of these discussions, both on the popular and the learned level, it has been assumed that authority is a something that can be possessed, can be gained or lost like a bag of gold, or strong muscles. Against such views, it has been argued through the ages that authority is a veil, a deceptive make-believe, that what is real are force and power, or power based on force, operating through constraint and command, and that authority is the same, veiled by a religious or ideological belief of some sort.

What, then, is authority? Or to put it more sophisticatedly, what specific phenomenon could one refer to in speaking of authority? For not the word matters, but the thing referred to. Our discussion has already shown that many kinds of things are referred to by the word. It might, in this connection, be helpful to look briefly at the origin of the word and the social realities which it was meant to describe. It is obviously a Roman term. What were the historical phenomena to which *auctoritas* refers? There has been some learned controversy over the answer to this question. According to the great Mommsen,[4] *auctoritas* is not readily definable in its original meaning. He thought that it had predominantly a sense related to a verb from which it is derived, *augere*, to augment, to enlarge. This derivation has been questioned and can no longer be accepted,[5] but that does not basically affect Mommsen's argument which is to the effect that *auctoritas* implements a mere act of the will by adding reasons to it. Such augmentation and confirmation are the result of deliberation by the old ones. *Auctoritas* was what the *senatus* composed of the *senes* possessed, as contrasted with the *potestas* of the people. The *auctoritas patrum* is more than advice, yet less than command. It is advice which cannot be safely disregarded, such as the expert gives to the layman, or a leader in parliament and party to his followers. This augmentation, implementation, and confirmation had religious significance, in ancient Rome as elsewhere. While it was not intended to set limits to the free decision of the people, it was meant to prevent a violation of what was sacred tradition in the established order of things, the assumption being that the people themselves would want to avoid such violation. It was believed that because such a violation was a crime (*nefas, Unrecht*) against the divine order, it might jeopardize divine favor. Thus, the maintaining of good auspices probably was the basic idea underlying the *auctoritas patrum* vested in the Senate. To put the matter generally and more abstractly, it was a matter of adding wisdom to will, reason to force and want, that is to say, a knowledge of values shared and traditions hallowed to whatever the people wished to do. There was as yet little of what our modern word 'author' implies.

These ancient connotations bring out the crucial role of reasoning in situations where men follow other men without being compelled to do so. When there are good reasons for doing or believing something, such action or thought acquires a quality which is otherwise lacking; it becomes 'authoritative'. What makes a particular course of action authoritative, that is to say, vested with authority, is that convincing reasons may be offered in support of it. These reasons may well be meta-rational in the sense that they refer to transcendental beliefs; we are at present more ready to recognize the reasoning which is so based than were men in the days of a belief in the limitless power of Cartesian ratiocination and scientific 'proof'. In a new rhetoric, Chaim Perelman has undertaken to systematize once more these often quite elaborate ways of reasoning and has shown how unreasonable it is to deny them evidential value.[6] In fact, it is this field of rhetorics which constitutes the 'field' of authority.[7] Whenever logical proof cannot be offered—the usual situation in politics—reasoning must rely upon authority. It is, I believe, the reason for Aristotle's concern with rhetorics that in a democratic or constitutional order (polity) people must be convinced of the right course of action by reasoning, and since logical proof cannot be offered, it becomes vital to understand and practice the art of authoritative reasoning, that is to say, the art of rhetorics. Rhetorics, Aristotle would define as the faculty of discovering the possible means of persuasion in reference to any subject whatsoever.[8] Clearly, to possess authority is one of these means.

These matters have been overlooked by that rather numerous group of writers and philosophers who thought they could build a philosophy of law upon force and power alone, as expressed in explicit commands. The power of him who willed something, was, they thought, what gave someone's decision authority. Hobbes and Rousseau thought, and many others still think, that the sovereign will was the source of law.[9] Much Anglo–American legal tradition has, by contrast, lived by the older notion, originally Stoic, that reason is of decisive importance in providing law with authority.[10] In this tradition, the judge becomes central; for he, a man learned in the law, lends the statutory decisions of an elected representative assembly additional authority; he relates them to the basic principles of the law and thereby makes them authoritative. In this perspective, the Supreme Court of the United States is the true analogue to the Roman Senate, and the advanced age of many of its members is not an accident, but central to its function.

A linguistic approach to the problem of authority in modern terms was attempted by T. D. Weldon. He remarks, in his *Vocabulary of Politics*,[11] that until recently no clear distinction had been drawn between power and authority, and that it is 'too simple to identify "authority" with "force rightly or justly applied"'. He then distinguishes four kinds of authority, ranging from pure force to unquestioning confidence, and on that basis asserts that 'force exercised or capable of being exercised with the general approval of those concerned is what is normally meant by "authority"'. Thus, if the followers want wickedness, they will obey wicked authority.

This way of putting the matter leads to the confusion of authority and legitimacy; for the latter means that something, and more especially a rule, is rightful, that is to say, just in the eyes of those subject to it. For while legitimate rule usually possesses authority, that is to say, possesses the capacity to offer reasons for what is being done and said which seem reasonable to those who follow the rule, the two phenomena ought not to be confused. There can be authority without legitimacy; for there can be a Stalin whose word and action were highly authoritative to his following; yet he may lack legitimacy. I do not wish to explore this problem of legitimacy any further here[12] but discuss Weldon's notion of the relation of authority to reason. At the start of his analysis, Weldon points out that authority somehow is related to the fact that he who possesses it could, if challenged, produce reasons for his words and actions. Such was the case of the Roman Senate, such is the case of the judge. So far so good. But when Weldon goes on to say that 'the proper use of force is always authoritative' he becomes quite questionable, unless the qualifying adjective 'proper' is given the meaning of 'reasonable' in the sense of the word or action possessing adequate reasons for him to whom the force or coercion is applied. Weldon introduces at this point an issue which is crucial; he tells us that when people begin to ask the question, 'Why should I obey x?' x is on the way to losing his authority.

When the question of obedience is raised, a number of answers may be given. First, there is the answer in terms of age: you should obey because x is older, is your parent. It is an answer in terms of status in a hierarchy. Another answer might be based upon religious belief: you should obey because God has commanded you to do so. A third answer might be: because x will make you a present, or even make you his heir. It is the answer in terms of interest and advantage. A fourth answer might be: because x loves you. It is the answer in terms of personal emotions and loyalty: you are devoted to him! A fifth answer might be: because article so and so of such and such a law requires you to do so. It is the answer in terms of law and the consequences of disobeying it: sanctions. The overemphasis on the last of these answers characterizes much of the writing on this topic in political and legal theory and philosophy; the other four are just as valid, and may or may not bear the burden of the argument in a particular case. The difficulty with the rebellious students in contemporary universities is that not one of these reasons, and not all of them in combination, will convince them of the necessity for obedience: they denounce the law as an instrument of oppression; proclaim their hostility towards their teachers and universities; they do not care for the jobs and other advantages society has to offer; do not believe in any religion, and laugh at age and parentage as old-fashioned prejudices.

The sketch of these rejoinders to the arguments in answer to the question, Why should I obey? illustrates what is meant by the breakdown of authority, but it also indicates the line of reasoning which arguments over authority are apt to take. At the same time, it shows the link between authority and power; if the person who is being addressed acts in accordance with the command at issue, then x has power over him, although he may not have any authority. The reaction of many simple-minded people in face of such situations of breakdown is therefore the call for power, and that means eventually the call for the 'strong man' who will harness the community's power resources to restore order (eliminate rebellion). Our analysis shows at the same time that the answers to the question, Why should I obey x? do not carry us far into an understanding of authority. The reason is that the elementary reasoning which these answers provide does not make sufficiently explicit much of the augmentation, the enlargement of reasoning upon which authority depends.

Speaking of authority in terms of obedience, as Weldon suggests, is the consequence of the close link of authority with power and the consequent tendency to confuse the two. In action-related situations, where the conduct of B as a consequence of a communication by A conforms to A's preference, whether expressed or implied,[13] authority manifests itself in obedience. This has led to the above-mentioned misunderstandings. For there is another side to authority, political and other, which can best be understood if one considers the analogous situation of the teacher, the scholar, or even the dictionary. Leaving aside for the moment the authority of impersonal entities and before considering the strictly political field, let me analyze the situation of the teacher, the scholar, the doctor, and the lawyer, in short the expert specialist. In their cases, authority seems to be derived from the fact that the person wielding authority possesses superior knowledge, insight, or experience. The authority rests upon these givens, which are accompanied by the person's ability to give extended reasons for what he decides to say or do. These reasons may not be conclusively demonstrable for such reasoning to be authoritative. Indeed only where they are not thus demonstrable is authority in the strict sense involved. Euclid's propositions need no authority to support them; they support themselves by the evidence. But not only such knowledge is transmissible. Even when the ultimate grounds remain obscure or debatable, knowledge can be effectively communicated. What matters in an authoritative communication is that there exists additional, and at times highly esoteric, information which could be communicated. There are additional reasons which could be adduced, and often are adduced when the request is made. If a doctor says, 'You must rest for three weeks', the patient accepting his authority will ordinarily obey. He does it, because he knows that if asked, and circumstances permitted, a medically well-trained man could give him elaborate reasons for this advice. Hence, the real question which is being asked by him who wishes to question authority is not 'Why should I obey?' but 'Why should I agree?' It is the capacity for reasoning or, more precisely put, the capacity for reasoned elaboration of a communication that matters. Such a capacity *exists* whether recognized by anybody or not. It results from other capacities which qualify an expert as an expert. The role of this capacity is particularly important in politics, because so much of what politics is based upon is a matter of conjecture, and of expediency. The contingent rules politics. The expert is a man who has greater familiarity with the contingent.

Involved here, and especially in politics, is what Michael Polanyi has so suggestively called 'tacit knowledge', that is to say, a knowledge which is not usually set forth by the knower. A man with a beautiful garden will almost at once find himself asked questions about gardening, and his replies will be treated as correct. Often, however, they will be quite disappointing, because he was not able to communicate his tacit knowledge. The role of such tacit knowledge in much science—knowledge which is difficult if not impossible to transmit—has often been overlooked.[14] It is more generally recognized in politics and such recognition is the basis of successful democratic politics: people are willing to entrust their affairs to a man who seems to them an authority without trying to understand his reasoning. The difficulty of subjecting foreign policy to democratic control is that it is one interesting and important field of such tacit knowledge and the role of authority resulting from it.

At this point, it may be well to return to and explore further the problem of the authority of impersonal entities. Among these, the most important for political authority are laws and constitutions.

In the case of laws, their authority is increased if careful consideration of alternative courses of action has preceded their adoption. Such consideration is formally indicated by the 'whereases' with which laws usually begin, as do resolutions. Plato, who was deeply concerned with authority as we have noted, proposed in *The Laws* that each law should be prefaced by a preamble, a kind of introductory statement in which the reasons for the law are set forth.[15] Such preambles have become the rule for constitutions, and they often outline the 'spirit' in which a particular constitution is conceived, as well as the 'author'. Thus, the American constitution declares in its preamble: 'We, the people of the United States, in order to form a more perfect union, establish justice, insure domestic tranquillity, provide for the common defense, promote the general welfare, and secure the blessings of liberty to ourselves and our posterity, do ordain and establish this Constitution for the United States of America.' The French constitution of 1946 (Fourth Republic) even contained an entire bill of rights. That is an extreme case, but an affirmation of the basic values and of the reasons for making a constitution are common enough.

Whether they are explicitly set forth or not, such reasons do in fact exist, and they are what gives the law authority. There may be several valid solutions to a given policy problem. In such cases, the explicit indication of which one one has opted for may make a considerable difference in the enforceability of the law or constitutional provision. Reasons of this kind need not be conclusive to be good reasons. It has been proposed, in this connection, to call such authority 'rational', in order to contrast it with an authority that is unrelated to reasoning, explicitly or implicitly. Such an adjectival qualification carries, however, the unfortunate implication that there exists, by contrast, a non-rational or even an irrational authority. This would be quite misleading, if authority is seen in the perspective of the capacity for reasoned elaboration, as is done here. That there may be a greater or lesser degree of reasoning, and hence of rationality involved in authority may be readily granted. Let me emphasize once more that we are talking about reasoning, that is to say, about the ability to argue effectively and at greater length about the particular law, ordinance, or constitution—in short, that such laws could be elaborated in a way that makes sense. The fanatic and the dogmatic man will rarely be willing to grant that this is so. An economist who is convinced of the scientific basis of a particular policy will be disinclined to allow that the opposite view may also be 'reasonable' in the sense of being capable of reasoned elaboration. The free-trade man will consider the tariff man an unreasonable ignoramus, and the goldstandard man will feel the same way about those leaning toward other monetary systems. But the position here expounded does not say an authoritative communication will be considered reasonable by all comers; it merely says that it will be capable of reasoned elaboration. By contrast all attempts at identifying authority with rightfulness confuse authority with legitimacy.

It might be argued that the authority of impersonal things, such as constitutions, is always traceable to the human authors who brought them into existence. That such authority of the authors is important it would be foolish to deny. But the difficulty here is that it is often debatable who was or is the maker—not formally, but in fact—of the law or other thing. In the case of the American constitution, for example, one might well ask whether the fathers at Philadelphia[16] are the authors of the constitution which is the basic law of the United States of America today. What of the long line of judges of the Supreme Court and other high courts, the members of Congress over the years,[17] or even the president: are they not co-authors? May it not even be said that the living constitution[18] is the creation of the American people? Consider the analogy of a dictionary. Who is the author? And even if known, does its authority depend upon him, a man usually unknown to the users? I believe that the authority of impersonal entities is comprehensible only in terms of the rational, the reasoning component of authority. Such authority is more easily analyzed in the case of authoritative communications of personal agents. Hence we are led to the conclusion that it is the communication rather than the communicator that is in a strict sense possessed of authority. The authority of a book is grounded in the soundness of its reasoning and that includes the reliability of its factual basis.

Reason and experience as embodied in a work give it authority. And through the writing of such a book the writer achieves authority. Reason and experience as embodied in a judicial decision give it authority, and through its writing the judge acquires authority.

There are, in short, power situations which are distinguished from others by the fact that the wielder of power has the capacity to elaborate what he prefers by reasoning which would seem rational to those who follow him, if time and other circumstances permitted. Such reasoning usually involves the values and beliefs, as well as the interests of the group within which power is employed. The wielder of power shares with his followers all or part of such values and beliefs, and therefore could, and at times will, explain to his following the reasons he acted in a certain way. It is a common, recurrent situation in all politics. What we are proposing is that this capacity for reasoned elaboration—an existential question—should be designated as political authority. (If that term is not acceptable, another one would have to be invented.)

A somewhat similar approach was urged by Bertrand de Jouvenel when he argued that authority is 'the ability of a man to get his own proposals accepted'.[18] But there is a danger here of having authority confused with power, for that ability may result from brute force. What we must ask is what enables a man to get his proposals accepted, that is to say, 'to gain another's assent'. Our reply would be that when such ability to gain assent springs from his capacity for reasoned elaboration, we have authority. It inheres in his communications! Only when what is commanded or asserted can be reasoned upon and defended is authority real (for the problem of false authority see Chapter 5 below). As George C. Lewis put it more than a hundred years ago: 'He who believes upon authority, entertains the opinion, simply because it is entertained by a person who appears to him likely to think correctly on the subject.'[19] Likewise he who obeys authority does so because he who orders him to obey appears to him to have good and sufficient reasons to do so. Authority is not an alternative to reason, but is grounded in it. The notion that authority has now disappeared often means that the holder of such a notion, without knowing it, is subscribing to anarchist beliefs.[20] Hannah Arendt's despair that 'we start from a fundamental distrust of everything merely given, a distrust of all laws and prescriptions, moral or social, that are deduced from a given, comprehensive, universal code'[21] results from the historicist fallacy which considers the present wholly new and entirely unlike anything that went before. Actually, authority has had its ups and downs, because the capacity for reasoned elaboration varies as a community is born, grows, is transformed, distintegrates, and is reconstituted. Arendt's view results also from an unhistorical notion that there was a time when all was well, when a given, comprehensive, universal code prevailed. Greek and Roman thinkers would be much surprised to learn that theirs was such a time. The uncertainty and the chaos which they sought to transcend in their thought was the reality in which authorities battled with each other, seeking predominance. The first paragraph of the first book of Aristotle's *Politics* points to the underlying givens and the overarching norms that are involved. *Nomos pater panton* —tradition is the begetter of all such community, and there can not be authority without tradition, nor tradition without authority. But neither is the opposite of reason, for both depend on rational discourse.

5/The Genesis of Authority: Value

How does the kind of situation which constitutes authority come into being? How can authority come into existence? Values upon which it rests, as we have seen in the previous chapter, constitute a necessary condition, but they are not sufficient, if they remain the same. The genesis of authority is the outcome of changes in values, and the collapse of authority results from their disappearance. Revolution is not an overthrow of authority, but the substitution of one kind of authority for another. In the gradual transformation of values (and beliefs) the authority of some men is weakened, while that of others is increased. The sequence of generations is manifest in these changes, and they rarely constitute a 'gap', though under extraordinary conditions such a gap may occur, especially in connection with war and revolution. It has been said that when the American colonies declared their independence from Great Britain, they eliminated tradition as a useful source of authority.[1] Such a statement is incorrect; for what they developed, namely the constitution, became almost at once a great tradition and the source of authority in the United States. It expressed the values to which the colonies had become attached. The same writer acknowledged this when he wrote that 'because those affected by the Declaration of Independence and later by the constitution have given their consent, these documents had authority;[2] for while consent provided a source of legitimacy, the documents became a tradition when their content was transmitted to succeeding generations. Consent was not an alternative to tradition, but the origin of a new tradition and the basis of new authorities. The values, once recognized as valid, became predominant and remained so. But they underwent a continuous change, and when Jackson and his followers replaced the silk-stockings of the Adamses, they created a new authority which to some extent persists to this day. 'The specific image of political authority, if it is sensible to discuss it at all, will always be in flux,' Jacobson wrote in reviewing the American evolution.[3]

At this point, the problem of loyalty arises. What does it mean to be loyal to something which is continuously changing? Who is loyal to the American tradition as embodied in the constitution? Loyalty can, in its deeper reaches, be built upon either love or authority. When devotion and faithful adherence are built upon love, the emotional side of a relationship to a political order predominates, giving it intensity but exposing it to instability. Love cannot be commanded; therefore another basis is needed for loyalty, and this basis is authority. When loyalty rests upon authority, the rational element predominates, if our conception of authority is accepted. The American constitution has remained subject to reasoned elaboration, and the courts, headed by the Supreme Court, manifest this element. The compelling force of power is thereby reinforced.

This decisive aspect of authority has been overlooked by those who thought they could build law upon will alone (see above Chapter 4, pp. 50ff). It is possible to say that authority's function is to relate laws and other kinds of commands to broader verities, to values and beliefs that transcend the particular judgement involved in a concrete situation. The complex relation of loyalty and authority, and the way in which they develop can be understood by considering the analogy from the family, from the relation of parents and children. It is an analogy that is often invoked by students of authority,[4] but frequently misinterpreted by over-emphasizing the power of the parents. In the beginning, to be sure, the child is helplessly dependent and in the power of its parents. Indeed, their power is absolute to such a degree that many legal orders have seen fit to step in and control or supervise this unlimited power to some extent. However, such power does not persist, as the child grows up. A sensible parent will gradually substitute persuasion for plain command, that is to say, he will seek to develop authority by giving reasons. By elaborating his instructions, he is replacing subjection by understanding. He will respond to the questions, 'Why?', and 'Wherefore?', to the best of his ability, and yet he may at times have to fall back upon power, by responding, 'Because I say so!' The situation may not permit a lengthy explanation, because of lack of time. Thus authority and power become interwined. The authority rests upon the fact that the child increasingly gains such insight into the meaning of parental orders and regulations; it becomes 'socialized'.[5] This process repeats itself in school and the larger society. All such discourse increasingly provides—or should provide—for participation of the growing person. He helps, so to speak, to shape these regulations and to make them his own. Thus discipline is replaced by self-discipline.[6] A similar process can be observed in connection with the founding of organizations.[7] Here the founder, often the 'author' of the idea to which the foundation responds, will commence by finding like-minded persons whom he can persuade to join him in working together for its realization. At first, his power will be great, because in the initial phase everything depends upon him as the leader of the group. But soon—and in developed societies with democratic traditions almost at once—procedures for co-operation—election of officers, etc.—will be established, and unless the founder possesses the capacity for reasoned elaboration of his views, that is to say, unless he possesses authority, he will be replaced by others who do. We all know that different qualities are called for in the founder from those necessary to the administrator of an organization, and personal tragedies are often caused by the inability of the founder to realize his limitation.

These processes, familiar enough in themselves, reveal the close relation between authority and values. For in the family, certain basic values are absorbed by the child in the early phase of socialization. These basic values vary, of course, from culture to culture, and some of the most serious conflicts in inter-cultural contacts are traceable to such differences. To tell the truth may be very central in one culture (e.g. German), while to be kind is central in another (e.g. American). This may eventually lead to conflicts between a German and an American, because the German seems to the American 'cruelly frank', while the American seems to the German 'lacking in candour'—dishonest! There is no point in pedantically elaborating these observations. The key point is clear enough, namely that the power of the parents having inculcated the basic values of human relations to the child, the parent is thereafter able to base reasons upon these values, and thus to become an authority in lieu of a power-wielder. Similarly the founder of an organization, who during an initial period has converted his associates to the basic values of their enterprise, is thereafter called upon to argue a proposed course of action in terms of these values, that is, to become an authority in their terms. Crises in a family—and in any other organization—are caused by shifts in these values. Children may learn in school what the parents did not recognize, namely values prevalent in the broader environment. This sort of thing is particularly noticeable, of course, in immigrant families, where the old world values of the family clash with the values in the surrounding society. Obedience may have been readily accepted at home, but appear in the garb of tyrannical oppression at a later phase. In organizations, changes in values may be the result of experience, or of obstacles encountered in a broader environment. Business firms engaged in foreign markets may pick up value notions, sometimes positive, sometimes negative, that were alien to them before such expansion; trade unions may impose restrictions formerly unknown; legislation may force a reconsideration of previous value orientation, as is now happening to manufacturers all over the world, as people have become conscious of the pollution of their environment.

The comparable situations in politics and government are derivative, but no less real. A party may find that its programme has become stale as its goals have in part been achieved, or have proved Utopian; hence the programme must be reconsidered and perhaps basically altered. Here the innovator must possess or acquire an understanding of the emergent values. This is more easily done by a younger person, and hence we find the authority shifting to a new generation. It is frequently incomprehensible to older and experienced leaders (and professors!) that the authority which they have commanded for a considerable time suddenly seems to evaporate. It evaporates because their failure to share the new values deprives them of the capacity for reasoned elaboration of a proposed course of action. To their following it no longer makes any sense. It happens even to very great leaders. Recent cases in point are provided by General de Gaulle and by Chancellor Adenauer. Their authority underwent a sudden and rapid decline when it became clear that their reasoning no longer meshed with the value preferences of a part of their following. In France, it was the problem of Europe that deprived de Gaulle of victory in the first round of the presidential election of 1965; he had not realized to what an extent French farmers had become 'Europeanized'.[8] Adenauer, on the other hand, failed to appreciate that Germans were no longer satisfied with his almost exclusive preoccupation with foreign policy, to the neglect of the most pressing problems of internal politics.

It is in these and many similar cases clear that the decline in, and eventual loss of, authority, and the corresponding gain and eventual acquisition of authority are closely related to the transformation in value and belief patterns. The entire dynamics of the pattern of responsible parliamentary government is intimately tied to these shifts in values and their impact upon authority. Relating this to our discussion of tradition, we may add here that the fading of tradition as it becomes more distant in memory is itself a particular and inescapable case of such value transformation. 1066, though an important break in English tradition, and 1215, an even more significant shift in emphasis, are far removed in time, and hence less potent than 1789 for the French, or 1776 and 1787 for the Americans. Both of these have become legendary, however, and have become profoundly altered in the intervening years. As a tradition becomes ritualized, and hence a symbol, it may gain in emotional appeal what it lacks in specific content. As it does, it loses force as a basis for authority, since reasoning cannot be based upon a symbol, except in rather vague terms. Even so, American tradition has not ceased to exist, as is at present alleged,[9] but it has, as we noted already, 'taken on new powers'.[10] There remains a central core, a stable pole in the shifting appearance,[11] namely the idea of a constitutional order and the rule of law. The basic values involved in these can, of course, be associated with a great variety of other values, as the provisions of laws and constitutions change. Thus, for example, the bills of rights of present-day constitutions display a very considerable range of emphasis. This fact in turn caused serious difficulties when the United Nations undertook to draft a Universal Declaration of Human Rights; this Declaration had to escape into vague formulas to reach compromises that were acceptable to all, but more particularly to the United States and the Soviet Union.

The stress our analysis thus far laid upon values as the progenitors of authority, true authority, as contrasted with commands and the like, expresses a political philosophy that emphasizes political co-operation and community rather than control and power. To an understanding of political authority as the capacity for reasoned elaboration upon communally valid values there corresponds a stress upon substantive values, as contrasted with an understanding based on formalistic ethics of command.[12] What this means in terms of loyalty is that loyalty to such a constitutional order can be felt only to the extent that the conflicting groups and individuals are able to identify themselves with its basic principles even when they most sharply attack such an order. The oft-quoted remarks of Jefferson and Lincoln in favour of revolution[13] are motivated by such considerations. The fact that loyalty in America is believed to extend primarily to the constitution which brought the system into being makes the search for an American conservatism so unrewarding; for constant change is a basic principle of this constitution. It inaugurated a tradition of anti-traditional evolution.[14] It is all very well to talk about the 'rules of the game' as a fundamental, but no clearly defined authority emerges from such a concept.

At this point it is suggested that there are different kinds of values. We have so far spoken of authority in relation to values, as if the concept of values were clear and unequivocal. This is by no means the case. No political analysis has been able to avoid touching upon values. The efforts devoted to working out a 'value-free' approach have failed.[15] The basic datum of politics is the fact that men value their life, not mere physical existence, but their communal life with all the values it implies and seeks to guarantee. This life is not necessarily the highest value, but it is the value without which there is no chance of actualizing other values.

Value has been discussed from so many different angles that its meaning is kaleidoscopic in its many-sidedness. Let us assert at the outset that value is a datum confronting man, and more especially political man. Value is experienced by the beholder as an objective datum; it elicits from him approval. It crystallizes in a judgement: This 'A' ought to be. And such a judgement has three dimensions which must be kept distinct: the datum in the objective world constituting the value, the desire or will elicited in the beholder of the datum, and the judgement expressed by him.

There are two primary modes of such 'ought to be' judgements. These may be expressed by two formulas: (1) 'A' *has* value or possesses value, or (2) 'A' *is* a value. Often people, in speaking of a value system to which authority might be related, fail to state whether they mean the first or the second of these kinds of judgements. Let me call the first of these judgements 'instrumental value', and the second 'inherent value'. These two terms are not dichotomic; for instrumental and inherent values are not mutually exclusive. Political, like economic phenomena,[16] exhibit both inherent and instrumental values. The relationship and possible conflict between inherent and instrumental values is at the very heart of all political phenomena. Such phenomena cannot be known without taking these values into account. It does not suffice to consider the instrumental values; especially for authority the inherent values are at least as important.[17] They are the basis of much political authority. But values are neither relative nor absolute; these terms over which so much ink has been spilled are misleading. Values are facts, given as much as other facts, namely through the experience of the person confronted by them. Values are never 'everlasting', as Plato thought, but they are none the less real. As such, they provide the basis for the reasoned elaboration which constitutes authority. Some value experiences are universal, such as that of life, and the authoritative rules derived from them are therefore also nearly universal. Many other such experiences are culturally restricted, and therefore can serve as a foundation for authority only in limited spheres.

In this connection, let me observe in passing that no highest value can be shown to exist, even though there exist hierarchies of values.[18] But these are strictly temporary, and their shifts have much to do with the shifts in authority. For what is effective reasoned elaboration in one constellation of values may fail to be in another. Available evidence forces us to conclude that no rank, no hierarchy of values, either inherent or instrumental, exists as a universal preference of politically organized men. They prefer to muddle through. The resulting contradictions not only produce many conflicts in political communities, but also rivalries over authority. Claims to authority may well be based upon good reasoning, based upon communal values, without being conclusive. The sharp conflicts over civil rights are only one striking instance of such divergencies[19] and the marked decline in the authority of the United States Supreme Court in recent years may be understood in this perspective. Its so-called de-segregation decisions[20] were based upon the argument that certain values, such as equality, were more important, more significant in the tradition of the American constitutional order, than had been recognized. The Court's authority sufficed to make this argument stick—a remarkable instance of the degree of authority enjoyed by courts in the Anglo–American tradition—and yet was not strong enough to eliminate all opposition. Indeed voices were raised demanding the alteration or abolition of the Court, not only in the public, but in Congress. Here and there, nullification has obliged the executive to employ force to en-force (!) conformity with what was now said to be the law. Power had to replace authority!

Our analysis of authority and values has shown—based as it is upon an existential theory of value—that the transformation of values, which occurs a large part of the time more or less gradually and without being intended, generates authority (and destroys it). This ongoing process can be explained and understood only if authority is seen in the perspective of the capacity for reasoned elaboration. For the reasoning is at least in part based upon value judgements. These value judgements—subjective phenomena—

ought not to be confused with values which are objective phenomena. Authority depends upon such existence. Their existence is perhaps most vividly manifest in tradition. Hence tradition is a vital factor in the effectiveness of authority. A strong tradition— even the dynamic one of modern constitutionalism—provides a firm basis for authority. If such tradition is either corroded or rigidified by dogmatism—the two go hand in hand—authority disintegrates. Perhaps the most important constituent of a strong tradition in the West has been the law. In the next chapter the problems attendant upon the relation of law and authority will be more fully explored.

6/Authority and Discretion

Discretion is a phenomenon of paramount importance to constitutional government, especially the democratic one, as it is indeed to all law. John Locke discussed the problem of discretion when considering the 'prerogative'. 'This power to act according to discretion for the public good, without the prescription of the law and sometimes even against it, is that which is called the prerogative,' he stated in the *Second Essay*.[1] He also asserted that 'the good of society requires that several things should be left to the discretion of him that has the executive power'.[2] Much later, Dicey defined authoritatively the prerogative in Britain as 'the residue of discretionary or arbitrary authority which at any time is legally left in the hands of the crown'.[3] While it proved difficult for the king to maintain such a prerogative against a prime minister backed by a compact parliamentary majority, it remains in the background to be used in an emergency. It will be recalled that it provided one of the main bones of contention between James I and the parliament, and more particularly in his quarrels with Sir Edward Coke representing the judiciary. It was an ancient institution in Britain, anticipating in some ways the concept of sovereignty as developed in continental Europe. King James and his counsellers, especially Francis Bacon, wanted to bring this power of the prerogative continually into play in all situations in which public welfare made it necessary—with the king deciding when this was the case! A radical spokesman for royal omnipotence, Crowell, declared that the prerogative was a special power and a privilege of the king. And although the king might, for reasons of political prudence, avoid the exercise of this ultimate power, there could be no doubt that the king of England was an absolute king. In a secret Star Chamber proceeding, in 1616, the king declared that he, the king, possessed, under the prerogative, power that put him above the law, and that the judges did not have the right to occupy themselves with such questions as touched the prerogative. That is to say, King James claimed absolute discretion. In this connection, James spoke of the 'mystery of the state'.[4] In order to vindicate such an authority above that of the law, James fell back upon the doctrine of 'divine right' and as such the authority rested upon divine law. It could not be questioned any more than the omniscience and omnipotence of God. Hence the king might, under exceptional circumstances, suspend all positive law by royal prerogative.[5]

It is a far cry from such extravagant claims to the extremely limited role of the prerogative today,[6] but what remains is the notion of the need of discretion under exceptional conditions. It is very difficult to account for such a notion—and Locke, for example, does not do so, but simply invites us to accept the fact —which contradicts the rationale of a government according to law. An interesting instance occurred when, in 1931, a weak Labour cabinet fell apart and there was no leader in sight who, under the traditions of parliamentary government, could have been called upon to form the government. At that point the king stepped into the breach by authorizing Ramsay MacDonald, though no longer the leader of the majority wing of his party, to form a coalition cabinet, after his Labour cabinet had resigned. It was at the time claimed by indignant partisans of Labour, such as Harold Laski, that the king's action violated the constitution; in doing so, Laski forgot the ancient doctrine of the prerogative, or rejected it. The course of succeeding events vindicated the exercise of royal authority. With our theory of authority as the capacity for reasoned elaboration, this and other similar occurrences can be explained and comprehended. This capacity is related to the idea that no authority can be legitimate, that is to say, can be believed to be rightful, which fails to fulfil the function for which it exists or has been created in serving the public good.[7] Leaving now the specific British scene and its tradition of the prerogative, we may undertake to generalize in the light of this tradition, and other parallel traditions such as that of sovereignty.

Discretion may be defined in various ways, but what is always involved is, first, the notion that a choice between alternatives can, indeed must, be made; and, second, the notion that such a choice is not to be made arbitrarily, wantonly, or carelessly, but in accordance with the requirements of the situation.[8] There is the further notion that discretion ought to come into play within the framework of rules, implementing them, carrying them through, elaborating them. Thus a court, when using discretion in imposing a penalty, is acting within the framework of the rules of the penal law according to which the criminal has been adjudged guilty. An administrative body, in fixing a rate, is acting within the framework of the rules of law, say that of public utilities which fixes the way such utilities should be operated. When a court or a commission or an administrative official acts in accordance with such general standards as 'reasonableness' or 'good morals' it is supposed to be doing this within the range of rules established by the law.[9] Such discretion may at times be abused and thus lead to a perversion of the law,[10] but a reasoning process is always involved which in fact elaborates the law and those charged with doing so must be believed to possess the capacity of fulfilling such a role. It is apparent that authority here steps into the dusk that is created by the inadequacy of rules which, being general, cannot allow for the specifics of concrete situations.

Aristotle had already recognized this problem and developed his famous doctrine of *epieikeia*, of equity as the corrective of strict formal law. Indeed it is the very function of the judge when he 'interprets' the law. The fact that such interpretation may, especially in the course of time, produce a radical change in the law, has occupied the attention of jurists, especially when discussing precedent.[11] It is a particular kind of discretion, firmly limited by rules and regulations which differ in different legal systems, but which always recognize the need for it. Codifiers from Justinian to Napoleon have always hoped to reduce the scope of such discretion, but have found themselves disappointed. For since rules must be stated in words, and words always are susceptible to a diversity of interpretation, conflicts are unavoidable and these call for authoritative settlement. The reasoned elaborations which courts in mature legal systems are called upon to give are an indication of what usually occurs, and an element of discretion necessarily enters. In fact it is because of this discretionary element that judges must have authority to implement the authority of the law.

To put this another way, discretion comes into play whenever no rules or principles can be (or have been) formulated, while at the same time no mere whim can be allowed.

For a concrete example, the choice of personnel might serve. A legislative body may lay down fairly elaborate rules and regulations for the selection of personnel, as is done in civil service legislation. There will usually remain some discretionary choice. The candidates may all be of a certain age, may all have a certain amount of education and experience, come from defined localities, etc. There will often be candidates who are identical in all these respects; yet a choice has to be made. The selection board may have to prefer a man from a certain university or not, they may have to assess the weight and meaning of certain letters of recommendation and so forth. The law may, therefore, give specified persons discretion to select one of the candidates. The expectation will be that such discretion will be used 'to the best of the ability' of the choice-maker, and that he will be able, should criticism arise, to give good and sufficient reasons, that is to say, will possess the capacity for reasoned elaboration, i.e., authority. The same holds within organizations between superiors and inferiors who are given discretion, and are expected to 'explain' by sufficient reasoning why they decided as they did.

What has just been illustrated for the field of personnel selection is of course particularly true in the fields of foreign policy and military affairs. Because of the highly contingent nature of military action, there is a tradition of wide discretion in this field. Under the tradition of the American army, military commanders have extensive discretion to achieve a goal that has been set. By contrast, in foreign affairs, ambassadors and other subordinates receive instructions on the basis of which they are expected to proceed, but not to initiate any action without such instruction. This divergence led to serious conflict in connection with the American occupation of Germany after the Second World War, as it does continuously in the relations between ambassadors and military attachés. The American military governor in the American Zone of Occupation, General Lucius Clay, considered Policy Paper 1067 as defining the goals he was to achieve: demilitarization, denazification, decentralization, including decartellization, and democratization. He believed that any means suitable to the achievement of these goals was within his discretion.[12] The State Department, on the other hand, considered him more or less in the role of a diplomatic representative, rather than a field commander, who should not initiate new policies without being instructed to do so. The issue came to a head in connection with dismantling industry in the American Zone to meet Soviet demands. Clay believed such dismantling to be at variance with his overall mission, and at one point, in the spring of 1946, declared that no more reparations deliveries would be made to the Soviet Union.[13] This declaration had considerable reverberations among the U.S. allies, not only the Soviet Union but Britain and France as well, and was bitterly resented by the men in charge of foreign policy who felt that they should have been consulted, at least.[14] The conflict was clearly one over the range and extent of discretion, and hence of the authority of the American military governor.

The question is also frequently the key issue in cases before courts-martial. The reference to superior orders turns upon the extent of discretion allowed. Courts-martial are inclined to treat this allowance as far-reaching; in trials concerning alleged misdeeds of American military personnel in Vietnam, the matter has become serious, especially as such an approach leads to the suspicion that 'the brass' is trying to escape responsibility for crimes committed in the execution of their orders. In many such trials before courts-martial, the defense is largely in terms of a reasoned elaboration of the decisions made by the responsible officers, describing the particular situation and the constellation of factors which induced the controversial action. The military have, in this tradition, a tendency to resent civilian interference in their work. They feel that being in charge of the defense of their country, any means likely to serve this paramount goal 'go'. Congressional critics of such military activities are seen as lacking in patriotism and worse. Secret hearings before congressional committees may provide a measure of *ex post facto* control which, by anticipated reaction, may induce the military to avoid certain kinds of activity. But such limitations upon their discretionary authority are invariably resented by the military who feel that their capacity for reasoned elaboration should not thus be questioned by people who do not know 'what the score is'.

Although the practice further down the line in the diplomatic service is different from that of the military, the same kind of resentment is felt by those in charge of foreign policy, when the Congress and the public at large demand to share in the determination of particular foreign policies, or the field in general. Foreign policy, especially that of a great power, constitutes what James I of old called the 'mysteries of state', that is to say, they depend upon an intimate knowledge of matters, including the proverbial 'last cable', which are not and cannot be known by outsiders.[15] Discretion must be granted on a very considerable scale, and is so granted in all the major powers, though with reluctance in cases where the policy issues at stake have wide resonance in the public. Here again, as in the case of the military, it is specialized knowledge and experience which provide the basis for that recognition of a capacity for reasoned elaboration, that is to say, authority, to those in charge.

In the case of foreign policy, there has been recognized increasingly the need for special training to lay a foundation for that expertise which is the only solid basis for authority in the field. It is the more curious that there should have sprung up in the United States at this very time a demand for greater participation of the Congress in foreign policy making. For most of the members have no authority whatever, possessing neither training nor special experience, and the congressional system of seniority preference in committee assignments prevents the development of a measure of expertise such as was characteristic of the committees of the French Senate and Assembly under the Third and Fourth Republics. When the drafters of the American constitution provided for the Senate's participation in foreign affairs, notably in the matter of approval of treaties, the Senate was a small body, and treaties were rare and solemn matters. The same might be said of declarations of war. Both of these provisions have been weakened by subterfuges: the treaties by executive agreements and the declaration of war by wars fought on various grounds without a declaration, notably that in Vietnam. To resore these two restraints would seem highly desirable, presumably by firming up the constitutional provisions,[16] for in these two fields the authority of the Senate would seem arguable. But a demand for participation of a body such as the United States Senate in foreign policy making would seem to overlook completely that only a small number of members of that august body would appear to have the capacity for reasoned elaboration, nor is there any method available for having them acquire such authority. If a body of the size of the original Senate, say twenty-five, could be popularly elected for this purpose and devote its full time to the task, it might work,[17] but there would still remain the difficulty of separating foreign from domestic affairs in the present stage of the world economy.[18]

Actually, authority is altogether limited in the field of foreign affairs. The general decline in authority which has been discussed is particularly marked in this area, because states are no longer able to provide the security which has been considered a mainstay of the public's acceptance of government. Not only authority, but legitimacy (see below Chapter 8) have been corroded by the threat of nuclear war. It is not certain that foreign policy in the classic sense is even possible under present world conditions. Actually, there is a plurality of foreign policies, but they do not form a coherent whole. When the Brookings Institution in Washington undertook in 1949 to survey the field of United States foreign policy,[19] it could identify 'objectives of United States foreign policy' and under its aims and basic principles it could assert that 'the broadest aim of United States foreign policy is the maintenance of enduring peace', but it had to qualify this statement by adding 'provided that the peace is based on justice and is achieved through the orderly accommodation of differences among nations'.[20] It also had to admit that 'the objectives of British postwar policy . . . do not differ perceptibly from those of the United States'.[21] The authors added that it is 'difficult . . . to be sure that they understand the basic objectives of the Soviet Union',[22] but surely the Soviet Union would insist that its aim is the maintenance of enduring peace! If coupled with the proviso that the peace must be just, we are involved in a basic conflict with the Soviet Union because justice is seen in strongly ideological terms. It is hardly necessary to illustrate these general observations; they tend to reinforce the proposition that foreign policy is 'authoritative' for those who agree on ideological grounds, but presuppose a detailed knowledge and experience in particular conflict situations: the Near East, South East Asia, Berlin, and so forth. One of the key objections to senatorial or congressional participation in foreign policy making is that it undermines the authority of those in charge by its criticism, without contributing significantly to its improvement. Men such as Senators Borah and Fulbright have been detrimental, not because they were evil men, but because they weakened the authority of American foreign policy makers, while reducing their discretion and thereby their freedom of action.

What is true in military and foreign policy is of course also true in other fields of more strictly domestic concern. For here too expertise is becoming more and more important whenever discretionary decisions have to be made. What has resulted is a 'crisis of democracy' which is inducing a re-thinking of its proper role. A differentiation of levels of policy making is in the process of distinguishing the several spheres of authority. This tendency is particularly marked in the field of foreign policy. In the United States it can be observed that certain basic decisions, such as peace and war, and permanent commitments (e.g. NATO) are arrived at after a wide consultation not only with the Congress, but with the public at large. The public will inject itself into the discussion and force an alteration of policy, as happened in Britain at the time of the Suez crisis, and is happening in the United States at the present time. There is, secondly, the level of interest-group involvement. Whenever foreign policies touch the vital interests of particular groups in the general public, they will activate themselves and, when capable, alter the policy in their favor. This has repeatedly happened in the United States, in Britain, in France, and in Germany. There is, finally, the level on which foreign policy is essentially conducted by the diplomatic experts in the State Department. A similar trend is observable in other democracies.

Quite a few cases exist in which the sequence: experts, interests, general public, can be shown to have come consecutively into play. This dynamism is responsible for the inconsistency of democratic foreign policy which has been critically commented upon, especially with reference to American foreign policy.[23] The discretion which could be deployed on the first level of the expert, in, say, the Near East policy field, had to be yielded to the interest groups from time to time (petroleum industry, Zionists . . .), and their discretion was in turn limited by the general public's concern over war. It is obvious that under such conditions, authority is very difficult to define and to maintain. All participants in the game of foreign policy possess some authority as here characterized, none possesses full or even comprehensive authority. This evident fact may well be the reason for the general decline of foreign policy making, and the increasing anarchy that prevails in international relations.

The discretion of a judge in interpreting a law and the discretion of a diplomat in handling a delicate conflict situation seem far apart. Yet they are both cases in which the role of authority is vital. And so it is in many intermediary situations. We have not considered the interesting problems of social work and the discretion which must be allowed the social worker who enters a home to 'help'. Nor could we deal with the many related fields of administration in which such discretion is vital, and equally so the authority without which discretion cannot function. It is possible to demonstrate that authority is particularly needed whenever discretion comes into play, and this is of course equally true in non-governmental as in political activities. Discretion without authority will appear arbitrary and generate resistance; this is likely to be destructive of organizations and create chaos in the field.[24] It is incorrect to say that there is no discretion without authority; for there occurs a good deal of it, but it is apt to become ineffectual in a relatively short time. Power of which discretion is a manifestation seeks generally to reinforce itself by acquiring authority, and it often can do so by a process of legitimation (see below Chapter 8). In any case, such authority broadens the scope of discretion, and thereby enables an organization, and more especially a government, to function more effectively over the long run.

Part III
Authority Rejected

7 / Freedom versus Authority

The attack upon authority has been carried on largely in the name of freedom or liberty. In these discussions, liberty is frequently left undefined, or ill-defined; also, authority is confused with power and associated with force, rather than understood as the capacity for reasoned elaboration. In order to clarify the relation of liberty and authority, we must, in the light of our theory of authority, state the problem of liberty more precisely. But before we do this, and as an introduction, we might consider a key passage in John Stuart Mill's *On Liberty* which is often cited in connection with our problem. At the beginning of his analysis, he wrote:

> The struggle between liberty and authority is the most conspicuous feature in the portions of history with which we are earliest familiar, particularly in that of Greece, Rome, and England. But in old times this contest was between subjects . . . and the government. The rulers were conceived as in a necessarily antagonistic position to the people . . . Their power was regarded as necessary, but also as highly dangerous . . . The aim, therefore, of patriots was to set limits to the power which the ruler should be suffered to exercise over the community; and those limitations was what was meant by liberty.[1]

Since, in his later discussion, Mill no longer speaks of authority, but of power, it would seem that he confuses the two terms, or takes authority to be a particular kind of power (see above Chapter 7), namely rightful, or power accepted by those who are subject to it. Thus authority and legitimacy are confused (see Chapter 8). It is however, historically true that a great part of the struggle against established government has been carried on in these terms, because the established powers claimed for themselves the capacity for reasoned elaboration, that is to say, the capacity to give right reasons for what they said and did— right in terms of the prevailing values and beliefs of the political community. Thus a particular authority, the king and the Catholic Church in pre-revolutionary France under the *ancien régime*, were identified with authority in general. Hence arguments were advanced against authority as such which were sound at best only against those particular authorities, and only in the perspective of the emergent authorities of the new age. For, of course, the partisans of the revolution claimed for themselves authority in the true sense as being the only ones capable of reasoned elaboration in terms of the new values and beliefs.

These remarks raise a key problem, namely that of 'false authority'. The contrast between genuine and false authority is often made by contrasting rational with non-rational authority; but such a contrast is misleading, since much true authority rests upon religious or other meta-rational foundations of an ideological sort which may well provide the ground for reasoned elaboration.[2] Crucial is the potentiality for reasoned elaboration. Not the psychological belief in such a capacity is decisive, but the actual presence of such a capacity. Only if this is clearly understood does the possibility of 'false' authority become comprehensible. It remains obscure as long as the acceptance of authority —what has been called the subjective aspect—is made central to the concept, is even said to constitute its nature.[3] Situations often arose when the capacity for reasoned elaboration—described as wisdom, insight, knowledge, expertise, in short, intellectual superiority—was believed to exist but when it in fact did not. Such errors are common. They may result from the change and development of the community, or they may spring from a deliberate 'faking' of authority, the pretension of a capacity which does not exist. Authority disintegrates with extraordinary rapidity under such conditions. But such so-called distintegration is actually the becoming apparent of an already accomplished fact. Genuine authority is present when a power-handler possesses the capacity for reasoned elaboration. The respect, esteem, and other such subjective psychological reactions are a concomitant, undoubtedly important, but not of the essence. They have often been asserted to be the heart of the matter, but incorrectly so.

The clash between authority and freedom has frequently been a clash between freedom and faked authority in anticipation of establishing genuine authority. It has been the appeal from one authority to another. Men caught in the particular struggle over the authority of their time have mistaken it for a struggle over authority as such, with consequent disillusionment. The early history of the Soviet Union is a striking case of such confusion; for the new regime was more radically authoritarian than the preceding one, and its authority is today largely unchallenged. Freedom calls for free choice, though restraints may be, and, in fact, are, regularly involved. The claims for freedom have usually been put in terms of truth. They are usually stated as if 'truth' were a clear-cut given, when actually much of it is uncertain, highly controversial, and can be stated only in elaborating the reasons for the position taken. Hence authority is itself involved in truth-finding and in truth-stating. Man, endowed with the capacity to reason (often misstated as 'endowed with reason') is yet a finite being whose reason is likewise finite and limited. An excessive belief in human reason may lead to extravagant claims on behalf of authority, as well as to such claims against authority. We saw at the outset (Chapter 4) that the anti-authoritarian criticism is cast in terms of reason, and it is true, of course, that the reach of authority is confined to the range of reasoning. There can be no absolute, no total authority, because there is not open to man any absolute truth or total reason.[4]

The relation between truth and authority helps one to understand better what is meant by false authority. It is that illusion recurrent in political situations when men issue communications as authoritative which are believed to permit reasoned elaboration when actually they do not, or do no longer, permit it.[5] For people may well believe that a certain communication could be effectively elaborated and therefore be worthy of acceptance, when actually the ability to do so has been lost by the power-handler, either on account of old age, or because new elements have been enfranchised, and so on. The falseness of such authority is revealed when the pretended capacity has to be employed, say in a justifying speech or a successful action. Thus the authority of the emperor of ancient China was believed to rest upon his being a 'son of heaven'. But if the dams broke or other disasters befell, it was believed that his capacity resulting from celestial descent had ceased. The problem of authority is at this point closely linked to that of legitimacy which will be discussed further on (Chapter 8). A regime, no matter how authoritative, which loses a major war, is in danger because its authority—the capacity to elaborate by sufficient reasons the decision to go to war—is in jeopardy, and hence its authority, and in the sequel, its power, disintegrate. There is nothing subtle or surprising in all this. 'Genuine' and 'false' are terms which customarily refer to the possibility that an appearance may be deceptive.

When authority is challenged in the name of freedom, it is often not clear which dimension of freedom is involved. In the drama of Richard Wagner's *Meistersinger* the young man's freedom to compose in an orthodox fashion is made right by ridiculing the rule-bound authority of a Beckmesser. It is a recurrent drama in all creative fields, and while very real, it does not alter the fact that 'only under restraint the master reveals himself'.[6] No art is conceivable without some rules which are accepted as authoritative by the craftsman. In this dimension of creative or innovative freedom, it is clear that the value attaching to certain forms, the 'style' of a period or a nation or a group, will possess an authority without which the style would—and eventually does—disintegrate. But there are two other dimensions, more usually encountered in politics, which deserve further exploration: freedom as independence and freedom as participation.[7] To illustrate, one of the freedoms of independence is the freedom of religion guaranteed in many modern constitutions. On the other hand, the right to vote is a part of the freedom of participation.

Since it is fairly generally recognized that freedom cannot mean that 'all men are (or ought to be) free in regard to all actions they might wish to take', since these actions might clash, being incompatible,[8] freedom must mean something else. This is evident in the case of freedom of participation; for a man participating in an election, or other part of a political order, obviously will find himself forced 'to play the game' by the rules of it. But even where independence is in the foreground of attention, philosophers have argued convincingly—and common sense has readily agreed —that each man's freedom must be compatible with every other man's freedom in an ordered society. The mental construct of a 'state of nature' prior to any society was generally believed one of great insecurity ('war of all against all') and hence contrary to reason. Freedom, then, is closely linked to power—indeed some thinkers have defined freedom as the 'power to do a thing' and hence became involved in the dialectic of power and its four dimensions.[9] For when someone, a person or a group, has the power to do or not to do something, to act or not to act in a certain way, he is said to be free to do so. Freedom may therefore be a possession, or it may be a relation, and it may be generated by constraint or by consent. The question of freedom, political freedom, arises in a power situation when the power of some participant persons to act as they would like is subject to interference by the power of others. Non-interference is therefore the elemental notion of political freedom. Whenever a political actor acts without interference from another, he is said to be free; and whenever he feels so able, he is said to feel free. This is an important distinction for the problem of freedom and authority; for a man might *be* free and not *feel* free, as obviously he might feel free without being it. A subject to genuine authority might feel free, though actually his behaviour is considerably interfered with by the preferences of him who wields the authority; his conduct is influenced by the authority. It is likewise possible for someone subject to false authority (despotism) to feel unfree. The rebellious younger generation in America and Germany is protesting in the name of freedom, although the young seemingly suffer from excess of freedom,[10] in a sense of acting in such a way as to damage seriously a number of other persons in the process.[11]

Thus it would seem to follow that both dimensions of freedom are intertwined with authority, though in different ways. The freedom of independence of a group of persons can only be maintained if an authority can set the limits within which such freedom is enclosed. The freedom of participation presupposes an authoritative order in which to participate. Clearly, as in the case of the freedom of creation, the other two dimensions of freedom can meaningfully exist only when authority prevails; for only then can the free be truly free, as they find themselves subject only to rules and interferences that are capable of reasoned elaboration, that is to say, rules that are based on persuasion and not merely on command. Putting the matter thus shows also that the complex interrelation of authority and freedom becomes fully comprehensible only when authority, genuine authority, is understood as the capacity for reasoned elaboration or to put it more precisely, as the capacity for issuing communications capable of reasoned elaboration.

The three dimensions of political freedom have in common that any interference by others is based upon authority. If it occurs on the basis of brute force, or deception, or any other form of manipulation (influence), then such interference means a limitation or an end of freedom.[12] It is therefore of the greatest importance in the interest of freedom that all power be clothed with authority. The confusion of authority and power has obscured this conclusion. The possibility of authority becoming false has further complicated the problem—for false authority is not compatible with, let alone promotive of, freedom. These issues are at the heart of the conflicts between students and the university authorities in Europe and in America. For the authorities have lost their capacity for reasoned elaboration of their orders and regulations. In other words, theirs is no longer a genuine, but a false authority. Under such conditions, the students claim that the university is unfree, that they have been deprived of the freedom guaranteed in the constitution: academic freedom more particularly. The response they receive is that they themselves are destroying academic freedom. Both parties are right and both are wrong; for the controversy arises from a misunderstanding of freedom, or rather the failure to differentiate the dimensions of freedom—the students are primarily thinking of freedom of participation and freedom of innovation, the academic authorities primarily of the freedom of independence—and a further misunderstanding of the nature and function of authority. The breakdown of effective and authoritative communication has led, as it usually does, to violence on the one hand, resignation and despair on the other. The academic community has broken down.

Some people would not be willing to admit that these are political issues, but they are wrong. The conflict has, on the contrary, revealed how highly political an institution the university is, and how impossible the liberal tradition which tried to isolate it from politics. When Wilhelm von Humboldt wrote his memorandum to the Prussian king, in 1908, he was facing a monarchy, just beginning to be constitutionalized, that emerged from the Napoleonic wars. Here the separation from the state meant detachment from the preoccupation of an autocratic regime; it did not work out, and the universities became instruments in the regime's hands. Even less could it work out under democratic conditions. The universities became the people's concern, and hence subject to the majority's preference. What had been John Stuart Mill's preoccupation in his essay *On Liberty*, namely how to protect the individual's freedom against the 'tyranny' of the majority, came to the fore: how to protect academic freedom against party interference, based upon majoritarian principles. It has been the problem of America's state universities for many years. The separation which Humboldt had favoured became the battle-cry of the American Association of University Professors. It was, of course, the battle-cry in the market-place of American public opinion, and the struggle seemed largely won until the recent student rebellions which, by their violence, have invited a renewed interference by non-university public authorities, exemplified by the the governor of California. Some of the defenders of academic freedom have suffered bitterly under this constellation. The freedom which academic teachers wanted to maintain as the necessary condition of their work lacked the authoritative support without which freedom cannot thrive. Thereby the intertwining of freedom and authority was dramatically demonstrated to all who wished to see.[13] As a consequence, some of the most outspoken libertarians have become the most radical authoritarians, and are ready to sacrifice liberty in an effort to preserve liberty.

It is wiser to stay with John Stuart Mill's conclusions concerning 'the limits of the authority of society over the individual'.[14] On a weak contractual premise, Mill argued that 'the offender may be justly punished by opinion, though not by law. As soon as any part of a person's conduct affects prejudicially the interests of others, society has jurisdiction over it, and the question whether the general welfare will or will not be promoted by interfering with it becomes open to discussion.' That is, of course, what is happening in the Western world today. Authority has to be brought into play to redress the balance. 'What I contend for is that the inconveniences which are strictly inseparable from the unfavourable judgment of others are the only ones to which a person should ever be subjected for that portion of his conduct and character which concerns his own good, but which does not affect the interests of others in their relation with him.'[15]

So far, so good. The only authority which comes into play is that of public opinion, and it is no mean one! But the situation changes when the acts are injurious to others. After reciting all sorts of 'moral vices', from cruelty to pride, Mill argues for 'moral reprobation' in retribution against an offence against the rights of others. But moral reprobation may not suffice, especially when the code of morality (the basis for reasoned elaboration) is not accepted by those who commit such acts. To throw rotten eggs at the rector of the university may be morally disapproved of by the town's citizens, as happened at Heidelberg, but such moral disapprobation will make little impression on students for whom the act was symbolic and intended to be derogatory not only of the rector, but of the institution and the system—the establishment—for which he spoke. It is quite clear that Mill's argument is valid only for a community that shares its values and beliefs. The authority is in a sense unchallenged, the offences are within, and not contrary to the system. The contemporary constellation brings out the fact that freedom cannot be maintained for persons who will abuse it to destroy the system which maintains it. To do so is self-contradictory. In terms of this discussion: authority is unavailable as a means of restoring authority and the freedom which depends upon its existence! Force is needed.

The totalitarians of the twentieth century have produced striking evidence in support of this conclusion. In the next chapter it is proposed to discuss the problem of authority in totalitarian regimes within the context of authority and legitimacy where it belongs. Here it remains to develop one general point of the problem of authority in totalitarian societies. It is the conflict between the attitude of those who accept and those who reject the regime. The notion of authority as the capacity for communal reasoned elaboration makes it possible to resolve this difficulty. In contrast to constitutional regimes where authority is diffuse and pluralistic, since authoritative communications issue from many centers of authority and not only the government, authority in totalitarian societies is strikingly centralized. Thus the authority of a Lenin, a Stalin, or a Mao is very great when confronting his followers, while the authority of such a leader is quite weak when he is confronting the rest of the people. It may even completely vanish: his capacity for communal reasoned elaboration becomes nil. We can say that political authority is both enlarged and reduced, as is freedom. The explanation is not difficult, if our concept of authority is kept in mind. The decisions and preferences of such a 'dictator' are cast in terms of the regime's ideology, that is to say, the values and beliefs embodied in the movement's creed; the decisions could as a rule be elaborated by extensive reasoning based upon this ideology. But they cannot be so elaborated for the rest of the people who do not accept the ideology, or do so only with many reservations.[16] Once more we find that freedom depends upon authority. The men who fought Hitler's wars were free and full of enthusiasm, if ardent Nazis; they were miserable mercenaries and slaves, if not.

In conclusion, we might repeat that the rejection of authority in the name of freedom is mistaken. A particular authority may be rejected in favor of the freedom of choosing another. More particularly, a false authority might, and often will, be rejected in favor of genuine authority. Such freedom will be readily granted in the case of creative, innovative freedom. It will not

in the cases of freedom of independence and freedom of participation; because they presuppose for their exercise an authority
which sets the stage for it in appropriate rules. In short, freedom
depends upon authority, genuine authority which consists in the
capacity for issuing communications capable of reasoned elaboration; and such authority presupposes the freedom which can test
such a capacity for reasoned elaboration, and reject it, when it
turns out not to exist or to be corrutped.

8 / Authority and Legitimacy

In common political language, authority is often confused with legitimacy. In their relation to power, authority and legitimacy are complexly intertwined. Some scholars have defined authority as some kind of power, for example 'formal power' or 'rightful power'. We have explored above (see Chapter 7) the problem of what makes people accept authority, and we have seen that 'acceptance' is at times made the central criterion of authority. This tendency has given rise to various interpretations of authority, and to assertions concerning its source. Max Weber[1] more particularly has in his discussion of sources of authority failed to distinguish clearly authority from legitimacy, and at times even equated these two related but distinct phenomena. He developed a tripartite theory of the sources of legitimacy, calling them 'traditional', 'rational-legal', and 'charismatic'.[2] He argued these sources in contrast to older notions which had been developed by earlier thinkers, notably Rousseau. For while the discussion about legitimacy goes in substance back to Plato, it was Rousseau who at the opening of his *Contrat Social* raised the question explicitly when he wrote: 'Man is born free, but always he is in chains . . . what could make this legitimate? I believe I can resolve that question.' Rousseau argued that it was basically the consent of the governed which could make it legitimate that people are 'in chains', that is, subject to government. Such a statement was a challenge to traditional notions of legitimacy, notably that 'the will of God', or an 'election', or 'blood descent' could accomplish the fact that a particular rule or ruler were acknowledged as 'rightful', that is to say, as 'entitled to rule'. Not so much theory as experience showed that success had often served as the source of legitimacy, success, that is, in establishing a government, or in making it work satisfactorily, and so on. Finally, there was the power of tradition—the fact that a government had existed for a long time, or 'since times immemorial'. This argument was central to the reasoning of traditionalist theory (see above, p. 26, Chapter 2). In all these explanations of legitimacy it was taken for granted that legitimacy was a 'good thing', that it was, in other words, desirable for a government, for a ruler, for power—and one might add authority as well—to be legitimate in the sense of being accepted, of being considered rightful.

In Plato's concern over *nomos*, his readiness to make *nomos* the key criterion for a good as compared with a bad form of government, the problem of legitimacy is implied. For *nomos* as right, as good old custom, would legitimize a form of government. If one goes beyond the specific setting of the Greek *polis*, he finds that the right or title to rule has been founded upon a great variety of beliefs, has been grounded in religious and metaphysical beliefs of a great range. The magical belief in 'descent from the gods', manifest in extraordinary powers of the rulers, is very widespread, from primitives to the high culture of China—and with some straining of the meaning, to the later Roman Empire. The belief in blood descent which treats the right to rule as analogous to the right of property, if not directly derived from it, as in feudalism, has been a frequent ground for claims of legitimacy. The notion that the ruler resembles as a symbol God on earth, has been accepted as a priestly reinforcement of both the preceding beliefs. The belief that time, that existence in itself proves the goodness of something has meant that prevalent custom and tradition create a right to rule (or to own!). All of these highly diverse grounds for legitimacy appear to be comprehended under Weber's one category of 'traditional'. The fact that those who are being ruled have expressed a preference for a certain person through voting for him in an election has been an accepted mode of establishing the right to rule, especially in 'enlightened' political communities; it appears to be the primary example of Weber's 'rational-legal' ground of legitimacy; for such elections presuppose some kind of basic law, or constitution. Since, however, the acceptance of the constitution is itself central to this arrangement, and since a constitution which has endured for some time becomes a tradition hallowed by time, the rational-legal does not seem clearly separable from the traditional.

There is, finally, Weber's charismatic legitimacy.[3] It is subject to even greater objections than the other two. The term was first generalized by Max Weber to account for some exceptional kinds of leadership. He mentions Moses, Buddha, Mohammed—clearly religious leaders, and indeed founders of religions. He consequently stressed that such a leader has a transcendant 'call' from a divine being who is believed in by the leader and his following, and who has called him to found a new community which will bring into being a new man. His leadership, his authority, and his power all rest upon this charismatic leadership. Weber then proceeded to generalize and secularize this phenomenon in two ways. First, he applied it also to inspirational leadership in general, even though not based upon a belief in a transcendant divinity. Secondly, he developed the notion of a 'routinized charisma', that is to say, a charisma which is no longer primarily based upon inspiration, but has become institutionalized and even bureaucratized—in short, organized.[4] The two extensions rather confused the analysis. In any case, one could argue (and I have done so[5]) that at the present time charismatic leadership in its original connotation is of minor importance, except in historical studies, simply because the faith in a transcendant being is not sufficiently strong or widespread to provide an adequate basis for legitimizing authority.

It is, however, arguable that in the Marxian tradition history has taken the place of the deity, and provides the transcendental point of reference. Soviet Communism legitimizes its rule by the materialistic interpretation of history, a belief which 'works', at least with loyal party followers. In the case of Lenin, it would then be a clear instance of charisma since he believed himself to be called by the laws of history to lead the world proletariat into combat against obsolete capitalism. Afterwards, this charisma was 'routinized' by Stalin, and since then the formulas of the Marxian theory have become ritualized.[6]

If such an interpretation is adopted, it conflicts with an interesting distinction in a recent discussion of legitimacy by Dolf

Sternberger.[7] He argues that the basic distinction is that between legitimacy based upon religion, which he calls 'numinous' (from the Latin *numen*, the sacred), and that based upon secular political belief, for example that in a constitution, which he calls civil legitimacy. For the Marxian legitimacy is a secular type of legitimacy. I am for this and other reasons inclined to dispute the interpretation of Communist legitimacy as charismatic. But since it is neither rational-legal nor traditional, a serious lacuna in Weber's legitimacy theory is revealed. Sternberger asserted another one, that of constitutional legitimacy: 'There is almost no place left in his [Weber's] system for civil government in its proper sense.' It seems to me that Weber would categorize it as 'rational-legal'. G. Ferrero spoke of this kind of legitimacy as 'democratic', as contrasted with monarchical legitimacy. And if Sternberger is right that 'it is difficult to talk about legitimacy in general terms' and that each form of government has its particular kind of legitimacy, this observation can be explained by recognizing the relation of legitimacy to authority. For only where the rulers possess authority, in the sense here defined as the capacity for reasoned elaboration, can they hope to achieve legitimacy in the sense that their rule is seen and accepted as rightful by the governed.

Particular problems are presented by the contrast between legitimacy and legality which has been argued in recent years.[8] Although restated during the Weimar Republic, this contrast was familiar to restoration writers after the French Revolution. The thrust of the argument is intended to suggest that 'mere' legality does not constitute legitimacy. It is an argument related to the ancient dispute as to whether an unjust law is a law or not, in the true sense. Cicero, St Augustine, and many writers on natural law have denied the character of law to 'unjust' rules.[9] In the tradition of sovereignty and the positivism associated with it, it has, on the contrary, been insisted upon that a rule adopted according to the prescribed procedure in a legal system must be considered genuine law, whether believed to be just or not. Accordingly, a system of rule or government which is legal would be held to be legitimate *per se*, whether in accordance with the kind of transcendant belief system, religious or other, we have just discussed, or not. The question of the 'justice' of rulers has been in the center of political and legal theory since Plato, although specifically he stressed *nomos*, as we remarked above, rather than *dikaiosyne* (justice) as determining the rightfulness of a regime. It would seem to be clear, in any case, that the question of such rightfulness is different from the question of whether a particular regime is according to law. In revolutionary periods when emergent forces stress different values from those upon which law is based, legitimacy will come to the foreground as the crucial question, since legality has lost its legitimizing effect. On the other hand, in relatively stable periods, the distinction between legality and legitimacy will lose its point; for whatever is legal, is inherently legitimate.[10]

According to official Catholic doctrine, the papacy is based upon the founder's explicit designation of St Peter as the rock upon which the movement he had started would be 'built'; Catholics claim a direct succession from St Peter to the present pope. The legitimacy claim which extends under the pope's sanction to the entire Catholic priesthood is a vital element in grounding the authority of the church. It is routinized charisma, and has proved its strength as a source of authority over the centuries among its adherents. But it has, of course, no claim on nonadherents and hence its value in terms of legitimacy is inadequate. Here the Catholic Church needs the kind of traditionalist basis which prevails among states. This fact may explain in part the determination with which the church has maintained its claim to the Papal state, no matter how minuscule.

The foregoing case which cannot be explored here in all its complexity, manifests the close link between authority and legitimacy as qualities of power. As we remarked above, authority helps to legitimize power and rule by the very fact that the capacity to issue communications that can be elaborated by convincing reasons helps those who issue such communications to be looked upon as having a right to the ruling position they hold. Indeed, it is possible to assert that without authority, legitimation of power and rule are unlikely to take place. If, in the Middle Ages someone, to be *legitimus*, whether ruler or not, had to conform to ancient custom, then such custom provided the ground for reasoning in support of the rule or ruler. Again authority buttressed legitimacy.

Looked at from the other end of this linkage, it is also true that legitimacy, that is to say, the belief that a ruler is legitimate, enhances his authority, that is to say, his capacity to reason effectively when challenged with reference to an action or communication. These observations, for which a great deal of concrete evidence is available in historical records and government documents, lead me to conclude that all the different forms of legitimizing rule in terms of popular preferences, whether broadly defined by ideologies or narrowly by such goals as prosperity, security or national freedom, are insufficient, if not reinforced by authority. Such an outlook is preoccupied not with what intrinsic capacity men have to govern, but with what performance they are able to turn in. The 'capacity for reasoned elaboration' is often tested at lower echelons of administrative personnel who are expected to demonstrate 'merit' through elaborate examinations based upon long training and/or experience. Modern 'civil service' structures, and the much debated 'neutrality' of such a civil service *vis-à-vis* political parties are related to this issue. The legitimacy of parties and of their leadership is provided by the constitutional order of which they form a part, but the politically neutral civil service adds to that legitimacy by its performance as well as its capacity for reasoned elaboration of the position adopted by the leadership. For such a civil service commands an authority which rests upon its technical and administrative competence. This is, for the large mass of the governed, the decisive criterion for the quality of government and its often disagreeable demands upon the governed.[11]

More important at the present time appears to be the wider legitimizing function of ideologies. Broadly speaking, people seem inclined, in this non-traditional and non-religious age, to look toward ideologies for determining what is right and what is wrong.[12] Therefore an ideology acquires a predominant capacity to legitimize rule, so that even regimes which have strong traditional and rational-legal grounds for a claim to legitimacy, such as the American one, are being reinterpreted as resting upon an ideological base.[13] Such interpretations depend upon a mistaken conception of ideology, one which is excessively broadened to comprehend any set of ideas men may cherish, regardless of whether they are programmatic or not. Thus, even plain nationalism has been seen as an ideology, though, in fact, it is not nationalism, but certain ideas associated with it, such as anticolonialism, which constitute the ideological core.

There can be no doubt that nationalism provides a distinctive pattern of legitimacy. More particularly in the newly emerging political orders, and earlier in the national unification and liberation movements of Europe in Italy, Germany, and the Austrian succession states, the most potent source of legitimacy was effectiveness in forwarding the liberation of a particular nation. Put in terms of leaders, we can say that figures as different in many other respects as Bismarck and Cavour, Masaryk and Pilsudski, Bolivar and the host of their parallels in contemporary Asia and Africa from Gandhi to Nyerere and Castro derive their legitimacy from their effectiveness in liberating and uniting the new nation. The two last named found themselves, however, persuaded to reinforce the legitimizing force of nationalism by a genuine ideology, Communism. They also found themselves compelled to abandon traditional democratic ways in favor of more authoritarian methods. In traditional democratic societies, the ideological legitimizing force is typically restricted to a leader's own following which he must seek to broaden after he achieves office. The legitimacy which his success at the polls gave him must be broadened. Imaginative leaders have realized this need. Thomas Jefferson's famous line in his Inaugural Address: 'We are all Republicans—we are Federalists,' has been echoed in appeals of later American leaders as well as in other countries. Party ideology will be soft-peddled, and replaced by national appeals. Nationalism will replace ideology as a legitimizing source of authority. In this century it has been possible, as a result of opinion polls, to test the result, and it has been found that a narrow majority at the polls was rapidly superseded by a broad majority in the polls; it was so in the cases of Presidents Roosevelt, Kennedy and Johnson, as well as Chancellor Brandt and Prime Minister Heath.[14]

The polls are typically cast in terms of 'popularity' and hence emotionalized. This is misleading and unfortunate; for it hides the fact that the party leader who has become head of the government acquired a vast amount of authority in the sense here defined. He could effectively elaborate by adequate-seeming reasons what he proposed to do. Thus Roosevelt—F D R—a great master of the spoken word, succeeded, by formulating striking phrases such as the 'New Deal', in making his reasons convincing to many who had not voted for him, and thereby in acquiring authority which helped to make him the legitimate, that is to say rightful, ruler in the eyes of most Americans.[15]

If such efforts at post-election legitimation fail, the legitimacy of the regime may become jeopardized or at least endangered. Anti-system agitation may thwart it, as did the Nazis after the indecisive elections in Germany in 1932. An interesting recent case occurred in the Federal Republic of Germany. When the then Chancellor, Kurt Kiesinger, formed a so-called *Grosse Koalition* (large coalition) comprising the former opposition as well as his own party, and leaving the task of opposing the government to the small liberal party (little over 5 per cent), the broad legitimation which had been hoped for in order to enable the government to tackle the difficult problem of German unification, a so-called extra-parliamentary opposition (*Ausserparlamentarische Opposition*, or *APO*) sprang up among dissatisfied elements, mostly of the Left, which attacked the parliamentary regime as such, and effectively challenged the legitimacy of the Kiesinger government. His well-intentioned efforts at achieving broad electoral legitimacy did not have the hoped-for response, and the *Grosse Koalition* failed in the next election, even though his own party support increased. It was interesting to observe how even those who had particularly supported the idea of such an all-inclusive coalition, such as Countess Dönhoff and her influential paper *Die Zeit*, became thoroughly disillusioned—that is to say, had to recognize that the coalition of the two major parties only served to corrode the authority of both parties in the mind of the electorate at large.[16] The contrast with the success of Chancellor Brandt in achieving majority support and widespread authority suggests that the dynamics of seeking legitimation is an important feature of the authority of party governments. If it loses profile, its source of authority, its legitimacy in the eyes of its own party followers is weakened and eventually destroyed. This result can be avoided in wartime only (or war-resembling times of international stress), when the authority, and hence the legitimacy, of the government is reinforced by the foreign challenge.

Summarizing and concluding this chapter, we might say that due to the propositions we have developed it is not surprising that the 'crisis of authority' has profoundly affected the legitimacy of contemporary government. It is not generally realized how marked has been the decline in the legitimacy of contemporary government everywhere. This patent situation is in part due to the fact that the rival regimes, Communist and non-Communist, are engaged in a continuous world-wide propaganda against the other, which in effect challenges their right to rule. In the Fascist era this conflict was even more marked, at least on the totalitarian side. Neither Hitler nor Mussolini ever achieved full legitimacy. It took the Soviet Union many decades to arrive at this goal. The sharp hostility of the Republic of China (Red China) to an international recognition of two Chinas is undoubtedly rooted in the realization that such a 'two Chinas' situation is a permanent challenge to the legitimacy of the People's Republic. The strong animosity of the Federal Republic of Germany toward any acceptance of the two Germanies is similarly motivated, although other motivations are more commonly stressed before world public opinion. This is natural enough in such cases, because a demand made by a regime in favor of its legitimacy already implies a weakness in its claim to legitimacy. Such weakness implies a fault in its authority: the reasons for its existence are contested! Such interdependence of legitimacy and authority is the most telling reason for clearly distinguishing them from each other, and much past theory of authority has failed to do so. The loss of authority of a political leader as he ages does not deprive him of legitimacy, although it may eventually deprive him of his power. What the careful analysis of authority and legitimacy shows is that authority is not 'legitimate power' as is often claimed;[17] for legitimate power may be without authority, a situation which arises in the approach to a revolution. This was basically the anarchists' challenge, and it still is. In the next chapter it is hoped to analyze the anarchists' position regarding authority.

9/The Anarchist Challenge

'Whoever denies authority and fights against it,' it has been claimed in a rather simplistic way,[1] highlights the anarchist challenge to all authority. Yet, one of the greatest of the anarchists, Pierre Proudhon, insisted that he fought for genuine and against false authority: all genuine authority is based upon the truth, he asserted.[2] Anarchists have also had an equivocal attitude toward violence; for if truth and therefore reason are the source of genuine authority, force and violence can accomplish little.[3] Therefore anarchists, in challenging authority, often are thinking of the particular authorities which speak for the 'establishment'. It may be the king and the church at one point, and the military-industrial complex at another. Although typically highly theoretical in their arguments, anarchists do not usually display any considerable sophistication on the subject of authority. Authority is, as we shall show below, confused with power and government, although among the most radical anarchists, more especially Bakunin, the authority of family, school, and church are as much under attack as governmental and political authority.

I do not propose here to set forth the anarchist doctrine in its numerous ramifications. The basic components are reasonably familiar. But a few prefatory remarks are in order. First of all, I should like to state that I am concerned with anarchism in its modern version, related as it is to the emergence of the modern bureaucratic state and the industrial society which grew up under it. 'While elements of anarchist doctrine can be found as far back as the Stoics,' it has been said, 'the first meaningful exposition could not come until the advent of the industrial revolution.'[4] I should like to qualify this apodictic statement. For its modern version appears in reaction to the beginnings of the modern state among the Anabaptists in the sixteenth and among the Diggers in the

seventeenth century. A good case can also be made out for Taoism
in ancient China having been anarchist, though Taoism seems to
be pre-occupied with the problems of personal happiness rather
than of social order, nor is there the stress on liberty which is one
of the key features of modern anarchist doctrine.

Such stress on liberty is, and this is my second prefatory remark,
also one of the confusing features, since a stress on liberty is
central to liberal doctrine. In one of Lord Acton's essays we find
the statement that 'liberty alone demands for its realization the
limitation of public authority, for liberty is the only object which
benefits all alike, and provokes no sincere opposition'.[5] Yet, Acton
is of course no anarchist! The key point is that he speaks of
limiting authority; an anarchist would speak of abolishing authority.
Even so, there is a distinct kinship between liberal and anarchist
doctrine. In the United States radical democrats have often spoken
the language of anarchism, in keeping with the anti-authoritarian
impulses of the frontiersmen. It was noted by de Tocqueville and
other European observers.[6] Some of the folk heroes of the Wild
West are out and out anarchists in action, and the tradition of
self-help and of vigilante activity is full of anarchic elements.[7]
Anarchism, like liberalism, exaggerates the inherent good-
naturedness of man; it is in the tradition of Jean Jacques Rousseau
and of some of the Enlightenment. Man is seen as essentially a benign
creature. Man was born good, whatever that may mean, and he has
been corrupted by authority and the impediments it imposes, the
frustrations it causes. Man can be regenerated by doing away with
all authorities. Men will co-operate willingly and spontaneously,
they do not need to be compelled into working with each other.

The third prefatory remark is to the effect that anarchism is
the extreme point of Western individualism; it may be called its
reductio ad absurdum. For the typical anarchist, his only concern
is the individual's satisfaction. Max Stirner exclaims at one point:
'My affair is neither God's nor man's, but . . . only my own, unique
as I am unique. For me nothing is above me.'[8] Other anarchists
have stated similar views, although Bakunin stressed the social
interdependence of men, and felt that liberty could only be realized
in confrontation with other men.

If one considers anarchism in this setting of liberalism and individualism as a thoroughly modern and Western phenomenon, its challenge of authority appears natural enough. For both liberalism and individualism have been strongly anti-authoritarian throughout their history. This antipathy to authority has often expressed itself in pedagogic theories. Progressive education was a relatively late flower of this tradition of challenging authority, and of teaching the young the need of doing so. Radical educational theories recur in many anarchist writings, which abound with denunciations of the traditional pedagogue who cramps the style of the creative young. It is an approach that has a very wide appeal in Western civilization. This is not the place to delineate the history of these successive 'liberations', but one should bear them in mind when considering the anarchist position.

The first, and perhaps in some respects the most philosophical of the modern anarchists was William Godwin (1756–1836). His major work, *Political Justice*, a classic in the history of political thought, is a comprehensive statement of the anarchist position, and we shall develop the analysis of the anarchist challenge of authority by concentrating on his work. Although not necessarily influential in shaping the thought of Stirner and Proudhon, of Bakunin and Kropotkin, he developed all the key positions, but avoided the glorification of violence which is found in many anarchist writings, especially those of Bakunin.

Godwin's philosophical framework is utilitarian. A follower of Bentham, except in his approach to authority and government, Godwin expounded a profound belief in the power of education. He, the first of the great anarchists, agrees with the last of them, Leo Tolstoy, that the right way of dealing with oppressive authority, that is to say with the state, is the 'censuring in the most explicit manner every proceeding' that a man might perceive to be adverse to 'the true interests of mankind'. For the 'revolution' that Godwin would be willing to favor, and indeed hopes to promote, is one by which opinions and dispositions are changed. One can hear the same sort of statement from peaceful 'hippies' at the present time. In a strict sense, this is no revolution at all, for a political revolution is 'a change attempted or realized by force [violence] in the constitution of societies'.[9] Godwin thinks in terms of a broader concept which includes a 'revolution of the spirit'. In the perspective of authority as the capacity for reasoned elaboration, this view seems entirely justified; for a basic trans-valuation of values is bound to alter in due course the authority in all reaches of social life.

Godwin is against all coercion. His animosity is rooted in his conviction that all responsible action must be based upon conscience and the consciousness as to what is right. Such consciousness cannot be brought about by force, but only by genuine authority, or as Godwin would put it, by persuasion. 'There is no criterion of duty for any man,' he argued, 'but in the exercise of his private judgment. Has coercion any tendency to enlighten the judgment? Certainly not.' Hence any conflict between such private judgement and collective judgement is purely a matter of force: he who has the greater force, wins.[10] 'Let us consider the effect that coercion produces upon the mind of him against whom it is employed. It cannot begin with convincing; it is no argument . . . It begins with violently alienating the mind from the truth with which we wish him to be impressed . . . One really punishes, because the argument is weak.'[11] While Godwin makes these observations in dealing with crime and punishment, they apply equally to other situations in which men are subjected to government. He vastly exaggerates the negative effect of government, and he underestimates the role of precisely that which we have identified as authority, namely the capacity for reasoned elaboration for authoritative decisions and communications. At the beginning of *Political Justice* he goes so far as to assert that 'government is an evil, an usurpation upon the private judgment and individual conscience of mankind'. He is willing to concede that it may be a 'necessary evil', but only because people are not sufficiently educated. He does not see that public business in its complexity exceeds the capacity of most men, and that it is not a question of 'the gradual illumination of the human mind'.[12] Hence he does not perceive the role of authority as an essential ingredient of any kind of social order, including a relatively anarchic one. The 'tribes without rulers' of whom anthropologists have recently written[13] are groups in which authority plays a decisive role, precisely because coercive power is virtually eliminated.

For Godwin the force used to *enforce* the law is 'violence' pure and simple. That such force may actually rest to a large extent upon authoritative communications such as are embodied in laws escapes his attention, because he is nearly unaware of the role of law in human society.[14] He constructs an almost complete antithesis between coercion and reason. 'Coercion can at no time, either permanently or provisionally, make part of any political system that is built upon the principles of reason,' he asserts, blind to reasons which may well be advanced for coercion, for example, in the protection of the weak and defenseless against the agression of the strong and aggressive. It is striking to what an extent such arguments on the part of Godwin and most other anarchists parallel Gandhi's philosophy of nonviolence. But Gandhi appreciated the role of authority in his very position as the Mahatma, and when he stressed discipline as essential to the kind of co-operative peaceful society he envisaged, the answer to the question as to who imposes the discipline is clearly authoritative and even authoritarian.[15]

The same contradiction can be found in Bakunin who could write, in his *Program* for the (anarchistic) fraternities: 'It must be understood that an association with a revolutionary goal, must necessarily be a secret society, in the interest of the cause which it serves and the effectiveness of its action; it must be recognized that the safety of each of its members requires a strong discipline . . . it is the duty of each member to submit to it.'[16] Bakunin does not openly admit it, but it is clear that such a discipline, based upon reasoning which favors the revolutionary enterprise, is the manifestation of a strong authority. And we know that Bakunin, a powerful and authoritarian personality, claimed such authority for himself. Kaminsky, in his searching study of Bakunin, has shown persuasively that Bakunin's powerful and emotional rebellion against all authority began with a rebellion against his father and family, and by steps extended to all other organizations. After a violent conflict, Bakunin fled from home—the landed estate of a not very successful aristocrat—and Kaminsky considers this the

definitive rupture with his class: 'Enfin il est un homme libre.
La grande aventure de sa vie commence.'*[17] Bakunin soon rebelled
against the university, and commenced his wanderings about
Europe, plunging into revolutionary situations with Utopian
enthusiasm, always expecting the new paradise around the corner,
impressing abler men with his inspirational magnetism and at
times urging them into senseless and destructive undertakings. It
is all summed up in a famous line of Bakunin: 'La volupté de la
déstruction est en même temps une volupté créatrice.'†[18] This
lust for destruction turns against *any* authority, including that of
Karl Marx in the Internationale. Much of his criticism of Marx's
authoritarianism is justified, and his forebodings about the eventual despotism (totalitarianism?) of the Soviet regime are spooky
in their accuracy. His rejection of all authority except his own—
and even that he becomes dubious of from time to time—is the
manifestation of his senseless and undiscriminating destructive-
ness. Such lust for destruction is linked to a passion for liberty
which is boundless, unequivocal, emotional. In his pamphlet 'God
and the State' he proclaims that the materialist, realist, and collec-
tivist definition of liberty is the following:

> Man does not become human, and does not arrive at the
> consciousness, nor at the realization of his humanity but
> in society . . . Only through education and instruction can
> he emancipate himself from the yoke of his instincts and
> bodily movements. But education and instruction are emin-
> ently, exclusively social phenomena [*choses*]. Outside society
> man would have remained eternally a wild beast or a saint
> which means nearly the same. An isolated man cannot be
> conscious of his liberty. To be free means for man to be
> recognized and considered and treated as free by another
> man, by all the men who surround him. Liberty is there-
> fore not a fact of isolation, but one of mutual reflexion,
> not of exclusion but of linking [*liaison*]; for the liberty of
> each individual is nothing but the reflexion of his humanity

* 'At last he is a free man. The great adventure of his life begins.'
† 'The lust for (or sensual pleasure in) destruction is at the same time a
creative lust.'

or of his human right in the consciousness of all free men; they are his equals.[19]

Bakunin sums up his thought by proclaiming that 'je ne puis me dire libre et me sentir libre seulement qu'en présence et vis-à-vis d'autres hommes. . . . je ne deviens vraiment libre que par la liberté des autres . . .'* He stresses as essential to liberty the absence of all interference or restraint; his human dignity which is no other than his liberty, his human right, consists in not obeying any other human being, that is to say, in not allowing his actions to be determined by anything but his own convictions.[20] His is clearly that 'wild and savage freedom' which Kant had excluded from his liberal concept of freedom, except that Bakunin's own convictions happen to include a passionate love of his fellow men which would restrain this kind of freedom by a mutualist conscience! We have discussed earlier (see Chapter 7) the problem of the link between liberty and authority and need not resume this discussion here. In any case, Bakunin's lack of originality is demonstrated on practically every page of his impassioned pamphlets. He does not and cannot recognize the arbitral role of government in the conflicts between men in society. For him 'L'Etat c'est le mal' (the state is the evil),[21] but it was 'historically necessary' as will be its extermination. For government is engaged in exploitation; exploitation is the goal of every government, the two terms are inseparable, and it is as true of theocratic, monarchical, aristocratic and even democratic governments. 'L'exploitation, c'est le corps visible, et le gouvernement, c'est l'âme du régime bourgeois.'† These sentiments are echoed by the so-called New Left in America and Europe. Liberal bourgeois thinking 'ends in an exploiter government of a few lucky or elected ones, and the slavery of the exploited great mass, and for all it means the negation of all morality and of all liberty'.[22] The sum of this raving is that 'all authority must be destroyed!'

This doctrine aroused the deepest distrust of Marx and Engels,

---

* 'I am only able to call myself free and to feel myself free in the presence of and vis-à-vis other men . . . I become free only through the freedom of others.'

† 'Exploitation is the visible body, and government is the soul of the bourgeois regime.'

so much so that the latter wrote a sharp critique of these 'anti-authoritarians'. What Engels had in mind, when writing this broadside, was Bakunin's rebellion against Marx's leadership of the First International. We need not enter into the well-known and widely discussed issue,[23] except to point out that it was basically a conflict over authority. Who possessed the capacity for reasoned elaboration in terms of socialist ideology? Both Bakunin and Marx claimed to have truth on their side, and each of them had of course *his* truth on *his* side. But it was Marx and not Bakunin who could make his elaboration 'stick'. It would seem that Marx understood the nature of authority! Hence Engels begins by saying 'Some Socialists have lately started a regular campaign against what they call "*the principle of authority*". They only need to say that this or that action is *authoritarian*, in order to condemn it'. (How familiar it all sounds!) Engels then says that it is necessary to look a bit more closely at this abuse of a term.

Authority, he observes, is in these statements supposed to mean the superimposition of an alien will upon our own. It presupposes the subordination on our part. Is there no means, Engels asks, under present conditions, to bring into being another social situation in which this authority has no longer any meaning and must therefore disappear? He notes the progress of industrialization and of combined activity. 'He who says "combined activity", implies organization. Is organization possible without authority?', Engels then demands. Suppose there had been a revolution, and property had been collectivized. Will authority then have disappeared, or merely changed its form? he wants to know. He then proceeds to describe a particular factory and demonstrates that the conditions of work, such as the hours and so on, will have to be settled, and the individual will have to subordinate himself to the rules. They may be the result of majority decision, and this means that 'the questions must be solved authoritatively'. Hence, Engels mocks, there may well be written over the entrance to such a factory: 'Let forget about autonomy whoever enters here!' 'To want to abolish authority in large-scale industry means wanting to abolish such industry.' He illustrates his point further with railroads and ships. Subordination, according to Engels, is imposed not only by the needs of organization, but also by material conditions caused by nature. Engels notes that he never received an answer when he put forward these arguments to anti-authoritarians, except verbal (semantic) evasions—substitutions of other words for authority. He then turns to Bakunin's argument that the revolution will at once abolish authority. 'Have these gentlemen never seen a revolution?' he asks. 'A revolution is assuredly one of the most authoritarian things there is. It is an act by which one part of the people imposes upon the other its will by means of guns and bayonets, that is to say with the most authoritarian means imaginable.' And he notes that a successful revolution must maintain itself by similar means.

It is clear from these passages that Engels misunderstood authority to mean power based on force, because he was thinking in terms of the establishment of his time.[24] He did not at all enter into the processes by which a revolutionary ideology is gradually 'internalized' and becomes the basis of popular thought, and that in the sequel the revolutionary leaders acquire authority in the genuine sense, as has happened in the Soviet Union and other totalitarian dictatorships in recent years. We discussed these processes briefly before (see Chapter 8), and might perhaps just add here that Lenin, in his famous pamphlet 'What Is To Be Done?'[25] proved himself a good disciple of Engels' (and Marx's) recognition of the need of authority.

The same may also be said of some anarchists, notably Kropotkin, and earlier, Proudhon. The former wrote in *Modern Science and Anarchism*:

> The anarchists envisage a society in which all mutual relations among members are not regulated by laws and by authorities, whether imposed or elected, but by the mutual agreement, and by customs and habits—not petrified by law, by routine and by superstition, but continually developing in response to the necessities of a free life, stimulated by the progress of science, of inventions and the growth of increasingly elevated ideas. No governmental authorities

then! No government of man by man, and no stagnation [*immobilisme*], but a continuous evolution such as we find in nature.

The stress on science, and hence, of course, scientists, shows that Kropotkin sensed the need for authority in the sense here recognized: there must be men and communications which are capable of reasoned elaboration. Kropotkin's work breathes a great love of humanity, a deep faith in human reason. His faith in the authority of knowledgeable men—scientists especially—is so great that he is convinced that coercion may eventually be eliminated and replaced by co-operation, by mutual aid.[26] His is a vision which resembles that of Marx and Engels at the end of the *Communist Manifesto* of 1848 and recently re-confirmed by the All-Russian Communist Party in its revised party program.[27] This authority of the Communist Party Bakunin would not have accepted. But he also would have rejected Kropotkin's authority of science. Repeatedly he denounced the idea of a scientific elite which he had come to detest in Marx's claim to have a scientific insight into the future. He wrote that 'the Communists are the partisans of the principle and practice of authority'. True revolutionaries are not going to proceed on the basis of a plan traced in advance and imposed upon the ignorant masses by superior intellectuals (*intelligences supérieures*). This was the central concept or motivating drive of this most radical enemy of authority in any form: 'Je suis un amant fanatique de la liberté.'—I am a fanatical lover of liberty.[28]

In conclusion, it remains to repeat that the anarchist challenge to authority either rested upon a misunderstanding of the true nature of authority, which the anarchists themselves recognized under another name as based upon reason, or it became self-defeating. Not only was Bakunin incapable of organizing the anarchists as an effective challenge to the Communist movement but he died an isolated and disillusioned man who on his own terms was not even free, since his freedom was not recognized by others. The final manifestation of the lack of viability in the anarchist challenge came in the Spanish Civil War, when the followers of Bakunin found themselves out-manoeuvred by the authoritarian Communists whose authority proved more powerful than their own.[29]

Part IV
Concluding Reflections

10/Tradition and Authority Vindicated[1]

Tradition and authority, Siamese twins in the history of political theory, refer to basic political phenomena; for there never was a political order or community without both. Our exposition has, I hope, made this clear and has shown that political authority is not something beyond or against reason. It cannot be appropriately treated as the opposite of the rational and the legal as the great Max Weber, whom many have followed since, did. For all authority is grounded in the capacity for reasoned elaboration, and legal authority especially so. When lawyers argue, when judges explain their decisions, when legislators debate statutes to be made, they invariably invoke the authority of earlier legal decisions, of courts, of legislators and of other governmental 'authorities'. Such decisions, the laws and ordinances and constitutions, are generally taken to be authoritative in the sense that they are based upon sound reasoning capable of extensive elaboration, should the need for it arise. Indeed, no legal reasoning has ever been able to dispense with such authority. That authority is in turn embedded in tradition. The greater the tradition the more authoritative the reasoning based upon it. The American Constitution, Magna Carta, the Corpus Juris Civilis, the Code Civil—they all owe their authority to their being embodiments of a political tradition. These observations carry the implication that authority and legitimacy ought not to be confused, but rather kept carefully distinguished. For legitimacy denotes that rightfulness of rules and rulers which enhances their authority. How could it do this, if it were the same?

Tradition has, since the ancients, been linked to the sacred, indeed the divine. It is frequently contained in sacred texts. The words are holy. Hence revolutionary activities typically defiled these very words; they are often substituting obscenities. S. I. Hayakawa has recently pointed out the close link of such obscenities with radical activities. He expressed his dismay that 'the radicals claim that they want a more humane society while they use a kind of language that makes humane relationships impossible'. If authority reacts with particular virulence against such linguistic abuse, it manifests the instinct of self-defense. For it is in words that tradition and authority are rooted; reasoning which is at their core presupposes the sanctity of language. Words are rarely mere words in such situations, and when the police use violence to suppress them, they are not 'over-reacting' as is so often claimed. Rather they sense the threat to authority and tradition. When the rector of a famous old university is being abused in gutter language by rebellious students, he has every reason, though often no legal ground, for expelling such students from the university. Such would, of course, be an 'establishment' reaction. Even an establishment may claim the universally recognized right of self-defense.

Tradition, when seen in this perspective, is a very fragile thing, even though powerful. A tradition is quickly destroyed and hard to rebuild. The great thinkers of the Restoration in post-revolutionary France could clamor for tradition, could in traditionalist arguments sing the praises of tradition, but such arguments did not restore tradition. What Augustine once said of the City of God on earth, namely that 'faith once lost, safety cannot possibly but perish also', holds of the political orders generally. Tradition once lost cannot be recaptured. A new tradition has to be developed to take its place. Often it is the old tradition in a new garb, but the garb makes all the difference. For the garbs of tradition are the words in which it is expressed. Traditionalism as the normative theory of the importance of tradition only appears when a tradition has been impaired or lost.

A political tradition is, to repeat, a tradition concerning the political community, its values and beliefs. It includes habits and customs concerning the conduct of men as political persons. Political tradition states how rule is conducted and how those who are being ruled behave towards the rulers; this includes their participation, and a possible 'control' of the rulers by the rules. It obviously has a vital function in the body politic. As a result, tradition has often been under- or overestimated; in revolutionary periods such as our own it has been underestimated, in the post-revolutionary and stable times it has been overestimated. Tradition's importance varies in time and place. Too much tradition ossifies a political order; too little tradition dissolves the community and its order. In recent times, there have been political orders with an anti-traditionalist tradition, such as the United States; there have also been anti-traditionalist traditions in political parties, such as the British labour party, and continental socialist parties generally. It is difficult to manipulate tradition, although the totalitarian societies of our time have once more demonstrated how much an autocratic regime can accomplish in this respect. A tradition, even a revolutionary tradition, can definitely and deliberately be built by those who realize its importance for authority.

There in a sense the so-called crisis of authority—that is to say the questioning of all kinds of authority, at home, in school, in the universities, in business and in politics—is a direct result of the weakening of tradition. The crisis is further intensified by the widespread misunderstanding of authority as power, or as legitimate power. When George C. Lewis wrote that he who believes upon authority, entertains an opinion simply because it is entertained by a person who appears to him likely to think correctly on the subject, he was still aware of the reasoning basis of authority; for to believe that someone 'thinks correctly' upon a subject means believing in his capacity for reasoned elaboration. But what is meant here is not 'scientific proof', but almost the opposite. For where there is scientific or logical proof, no authority is needed. Even the most stupid or silly man who states that two and two make four will not be questioned. But when the same man states that 'democracy is the best', or even a good, form of government, nobody will listen to him. Reasoning upon values—in many ways the most important kind of reasoning there is—demands authority.

In a most interesting detailed study of the popular sources of political authority in which Oscar and Mary Handlin analyzed the processes by which the Massachusetts Constitution was adopted by extended argument,[2] the authors were able to show that the process was a revolutionary one. 'The men who effected the change were as informed as those of any Western nation about the abstract ideas of natural rights, constitutions and liberty.' The new authority which arose in the course of this struggle was based upon reasoning that related what was happening to these values. The documents which the authors gathered 'reveal the popular involvement in the constitution-making process'. They also reveal how authority shifted from one kind of reasoning to another. The authority of the king's servants collapsed almost overnight, and new and often unknown men took their place, because they possessed the capacity for reasoned elaboration of what they proposed. These extraordinary documents illustrate in a striking way the transition from one authority to another. They demonstrate vividly the crucial role of reasoning in situations where men follow other men without being compelled to do so. We can see here what we showed in Chapter 4, namely that when there are good reasons for doing or believing something, such action or thought acquires a quality which is otherwise lacking: it becomes authoritative. Convincing reasons can be offered in support of it. Rhetorics, therefore, constitutes the field of authority. Whenever logical proof—so-called scientific proof—cannot be offered—the usual situation in politics—reasoning must rely upon authority. Aristotle knew it, and therefore having opted for constitutional government, he had to acknowledge the vital importance of rhetorics, as contrasted with dialectics. For rhetorics is according to him the faculty for discovering the possible means of persuasion in reference to any subject whatever.

When considered in this perspective, it becomes apparent that authority is quite distinct from the employment of force which is usually implied in the notion of 'authoritarianism'. It is possible to put the matter thus: authoritarianism consists in the arbitrary uses to which false authority puts resources other than persuasion in making people do what it wants them to do. When the authors-editors of a recent volume on one-party systems decided to present their findings under the heading of *Authoritarian Politics*,[3] they in a sense contradicted their own findings. For they showed that in these systems, authority, genuine authority as we understand it was weak. Much of the evidence also tended to suggest that such lack of authority was a source of weakness. The introductory essay significantly concludes: 'As in any relatively stable political order, procedural regularity furnishes the dissenter with his opportunity and his opiate. In an established single party system, as in the democratic competitive system, political stability is measured by the degree to which the system possesses the institutional channels for transforming dissenters into participants.'[4] What this means of course is that power is reinforced by authority, that is that those who hold power acquire the capacity for reasoned elaboration. This has happened in the Soviet Union since the death of Stalin.

Thomas Hobbes defined authority as 'the right of doing any action'.[5] Thus he adopted a position which is still widely held namely that authority is rightful power. He adds later that 'no man is obliged by a covenant whereof he is not author'. Authority is for him explainable in terms that link it to authorizing, or instructing someone to action on behalf of the authorizer. At other points he speaks of 'authority of scripture', and similar relationships. If one gives a person the right to act on one's behalf, he authorizes such action. These are meanings which still are widely employed. But if one inquires further into what behavioral implications are implied in such 'rights'—intrinsically a normative terms—he finds that there is typically meant to be given to the agent that which enables him to elaborate upon the specific proposal. This sort of relationship is common in the dealings of nations with each other. An ambassador is characteristically a man who has learned how to elaborate, often by intricate reasoning, upon the intention of his principal. It is part of his diplomatic skill to do so without going beyond the authorization he has. This may at times be very difficult or even impossible. When Chancellor Brandt sent an envoy to Moscow to open the negotiations with the Soviet Union for improving Soviet–German relations, that envoy was chosen in part because he was believed to possess to a certain extent the confidence of the Soviet leadership, and could therefore be effective in elaborating upon the reasons for the new approach, whereas one who was known to be anti-Soviet in his general outlook would not have been believed and therefore would not possess the capacity for reasoned elaboration of such a proposal. Such situations are recurrent, and the mere 'right' to speak for the German leader would not have sufficed; it would have been some kind of authority, but not full and genuine. This became clear when the same man was sent to Washington to explain the position of the German government, but failed, because he did not have that degree of authority, and others, including the chancellor himself, had to go and repair the damage. This example is one of many that could be given for the great role which authority plays in international relations.

The limits of Hobbes' understanding of the phenomenon of authority are occasioned by his overstress upon power as the basis of politics. When he succinctly stated that 'law is a command' he revealed this misunderstanding. For law, while often a command, is by no means always such. Most customary law is not that, and Hobbes had to undertake a rather forced explanation. 'Seeing then,' he wrote in discussing law, 'all laws written and unwritten, have their *authority, and force,* from the will of the Commonwealth . . . the reason of this our artificial man and commonwealth, and his command [it is] that makes law.'[6] And in developing his argument, he concludes that 'the authority of the law . . . consists in the command of the sovereign only'. Thus the law of nature as discovered by reason is not law except by authority of the sovereign. For the interpretation of all law is by authority of the sovereign, and 'all laws, written and unwritten, have need of interpretation'. And he observes that 'the interpretation of the law of nature, is the sentence of the judge constituted by the sovereign authority'.[7] These opinions of the philosopher of absolute power, of authority as rightful power, show that those who in modern jurisprudence have taken these positions are Hobbesians, are radical positivists who do not allow any standard by which to assess the actions of the sovereign for practical purposes. The radical authoritarianism implied in this position is by no means 'totalitarian', even though the totalitarians are among other things also such authoritarians.

Edmund Burke, the great traditionalist, does not deal at length with authority, although the notion of it is implicit in much that he wrote and said. No human authority can dispense with 'the eternal laws of Him that gave power' he proclaimed in his 'Speech on the Impeachment of Warren Hastings',[8] in 1788.

Hence 'a law directed against the mass of the nation has not the nature of a reasonable institution, so neither has it the authority; for in all forms of government the people is the true legislator . . . the remote and efficient cause [of a law] is the consent of the people, either actual or implied; and such consent is absolutely essential to its validity . . . two things are essentially requisite: first a proper and sufficient human power', and 'second such a fit and equitable constitution as they have a right to declare and render binding'. Hence in Burke's view the authority is derived from the people's consent. It is evident from these and other similar passages that Burke felt clearly the need for authority which is exemplified in the capacity for reasoned elaboration of the principles upon which it is based. When in his *Reflections on the French Revolution* he stated his often-cited conviction that the state 'is a partnership in all science, a partnership in all art, a partnership in every virtue and in all perfection—a partnership not only between those who are living, but between those who are living, those who are dead and those who are to be born', he circumscribed at the same time the basis of all authority as he saw it.[9] 'No man carries further than I do the policy of making government pleasing to the people,' and being that gives it authority, in Burke's view, but only within the limits of natural law. For it is natural law that buttresses genuine authority for him. He would never consent to such a statement as can be found in contemporary writings that 'force exercised or capable of being exercised with the general approval of those concerned is what is normally meant by "authority" '.[10] For authority is not above the law of nature, but based upon it.

De Maistre and other writers of the traditionalist and authoritarian reaction to the French revolution went to exaggerated length in stressing the non-rational character of authority. We have seen how de Maistre wished to liquidate the entire tradition of the Enlightenment, and one could perhaps even say of scientific modernism. In seeking a basis for so extravagant an authority claim, he found himself obliged to fall back upon religion, and more especially Christianity in its Roman Catholic version. In his *Du Pape*, in which he undertook to justify the claim of infallibility for the pope in doctrinal matters, he speaks of authority in very normative terms; not what it is, but what it ought to be is his concern. To be sure, Burke had insisted that the source of all authority is God. It meant that the political authority is tied to and dependent upon moral authority. The faith or belief prevalent in a given society provides the basis for all authority. We might add that this is true whether one understands authority as 'rightful rule' or as the 'capacity for reasoned elaboration'.

The word 'authority' as such is not important in the writings of de Maistre and his sympathizers. But the whole of his work is permeated by the sense of authority, especially in such discussions as that of the question of papal supremacy and whether the popes are above councils or not. The latter question, indeed, he considers meaningless, since there can be no council without a pope who must call it, and who can dissolve it.[11] Such a radical *ipse dixit* view of authority, dubious enough in the field of religion where it is recurrent especially among founders of religions, was bound to produce a sharp reaction. This reaction was carried to an extreme by the anarchists. For all of them, authority was the point of most explicit rejection. Godwin no less than Stirner, and Proudhon no less than Bakunin and Kropotkin never weary of denouncing authority. None, however, undertakes to clarify what they wish to be understood by this demonic something; yet it is clear that they are inclined to follow conventional usage in taking it to mean power—but of course not 'rightful' power. On the contrary, it is a basic theme of all anarchist writings that 'all authority is bad'. It is directly related to anarchist glorification of liberty which is the absolute good. The spontaneity and creativity of action can be found only in free action which is freely inspired; every inhibition is evil and must be removed, in all areas of life, but more especially in political life. Whether the particular anarchist believes in destroying authority by enlightened

education, or by violence, he is certain beyond the cavil of a doubt
that it must be destroyed. Anarchists become entangled in contradictions, when applying this principle to their own activity.
The sad failure which so many of them experience is traceable
to their incapacity to build organizations, because they cannot be
fashioned without authority. This inner contradiction is particularly
dramatic in the case of the famous conflict between Bakunin and
Marx. It would lead too far afield to document these statements
by extended references to anarchist writings, and it seems un-
necessary, since this drama is unfolding before our eyes in the
radical youth and student movements of our time. Philosophically,
the anarchist argument rests upon an assumed 'goodness of human
nature', and of nature in general; hence also the equality of all
men. Authority, even if understood as the capacity for reasoned
elaboration, rests upon the contrary assumption that men are un-
equal in this respect, and that 'goodness' cannot be specified,
except in terms of values which imply this capacity for reasoning.
Authority and liberty are, therefore, not antithetical, but comple-
mentary. Only a measure of order which authority makes possible
will enable men to enjoy a degree of liberty. There can be no
authority without liberty, as there can be no liberty without
authority, and to juxtapose them is to falsify both. Authoritarians
and anarchists are both destructive of liberty and of authority.

However, a serious misunderstanding may arise from such a
statement, if one does not distinguish between genuine and false
authority. A particular authority may, as we said earlier (Chapter
7), be rejected in favor of the freedom of choosing another. More
particularly a false authority might, and often will, be rejected
in favor of genuine authority. Such freedom will be readily granted
in the case of creative, innovative freedom. It will not usually be
so granted in the cases of freedom of independence and of participation; for they presuppose for their exercise an authority which
sets the stage for such freedom in appropriate rules.

In any case, corroded authority cannot be re-established by
force. A return to what had been authority before the challenge
is almost always futile. The restorations of European history show
it. The belief, widespread in European academic circles, that

academic authority, undermined by student rebellions, can be restored by governmental fiat, is likely to prove abortive. Hence the outlook for the universities is depressing. How can a school of higher learning hope to function effectively without the authority of those who are to transmit tradition and show its creative potential for further development? That a great tradition can be created, Humboldt's reforms and the founding of the University of Berlin demonstrate as clearly as do the American universities. But such an act presupposes a deep-seated belief, on the part of those who are to accept it, in the principles upon which it is founded. Is anyone ready at this time to proclaim such a belief? Thoreau put it rather well, when he spoke of the seed-time of character we must have, if we are to look for a harvest of ideas. Continuing this simile, a harvest of authority and of the tradition upon which it is built can only be hoped for when there has been a seed-time of deep-seated faith.

Notes
and
References

1/Tradition as Fact and Norm

1 Max Weber, *Wirtschaft und Gesellschaft*, 2nd edn, 1925, chap. I, pp. 145 ff. An English translation is found in *Max Weber: The Theory of Social and Economic Organization*, trs. by A. M. Henderson and Talcott Parsons, ed. and intro. Talcott Parsons, 1947, pp. 56 ff.

2 Charles S. Pierce, 'How to Make our Ideas Clear' as reprinted in *Love, Chance, and Logic*, 1923, p. 55.

3 Aristotle, *Rhetorics*, Ch. Perelman and L. Olbrechts-Tyteca, *The New Rhetoric—A Treatise on Argumentation*, 1969, pp. 166 ff. The French original was published in 1958—the argument is present throughout the volume. Cf. my review article in *The Natural Law Forum*, Vol. 7, 1962, pp. 199 ff.

4 Adolf Harnack, *Lehrbuch der Dogmengeschichte*, 3 vols., 1885, 1897. In English translation by Neil Buchanan under the title *History of Dogma*, reprinted by Dover, 1961 (3rd German edn.), Vol. III, pp. 207 ff. (English edn).

5 I. Lloyd and Suzanne Hoeber Rudolph, *The Modernity of Tradition*, 1967, p. 3.

6 Sir Edward Coke, Introduction to the Fourth Book of the *Institutes*. For background see Roscoe Pound, *An Introduction to the Philosophy of Law*, 1922, and my *Man and His Government*, 1963, chaps. 14 and 15.

7 See my *The Philosophy of Law in Historical Perspective*, pp. 79 ff. Also *Constitutional Government and Democracy*, 4th edn, 1968, chap. VI.

8 Sir Edward Coke, *Reports*, Vol. XII, pp. 64–5.

9 See my paper 'On Rereading Machiavelli and Althusius: Reason, Rationality and Religion', in *Rational Decision—Nomos* VII, 1964, pp. 177 ff.

10 Harnack, op. cit. (note 4 above).

11 Max Radin, in his article on tradition in the *Encyclopedia of the Social Sciences*, defined tradition as 'not a mere fact like an existing custom, nor a story that exhausts its significance in being told; it is an idea which expresses a value judgment'.

12 See for example the extensive discussion of *concordia* in Johannes Althusius' *Politica Methodice Digesta*, 3rd edn, 1614, chap. XXXI. See also the introduction to my edition of 1930.

13 The rangy issues of ideology are explored from many different view-points in *Annales de la Philosophie Politique*, Vol. 9, 1971. See also chap. 4 of my work cited in note 6 above.

14 See my *Totalitarian Dictatorship and Autocracy*, 2nd edn, 1965, chaps. 7–9, esp. at pp. 111–12.

15 Gabriel A. Almond and James S. Coleman (eds.), *The Politics of the Developing Areas*, 1960, p. 27 (by Almond).

16 Judith N. Sklar, *Men and Citizens—A Study of Rousseau's Social Theory*, 1969, esp. pp. 144 ff., and J. J. Rousseau, *Emile*, Book IV.

17 Rousseau, *Contrat Social*, Book II, chap. 12.

18 Cf. Charles E. Merriam, *The Making of Citizens*, 1931. The treatment is conventional, though the work was pathfinding. In present day jargon, these matters are discussed under the heading of 'socialization'.

19 On anomie, Emile Durkheim, *Le Suicide*, 1897, summarized in Sebastian de Grazia, *The Political Community*, 1948, pp. 3–5. De Grazia's entire volume is preoccupied with the problem of anomie.

20 Albert Somit and Joseph Tanenhaus, in their *American Political Science— A Profile of a Discipline*, 1964, esp. pp. 65 ff. do not stress this distinction, but their general outlook is demonstrably anti-traditionalist. In their more recent *The Development of Political Science*, 1967, they would date the beginnings to the late nineteenth century. I myself would plead for Aristotle as the basis of tradition in political science; see my *Die Politische Wissenschaft*, 1961.

21 See on this my work, cited in note 7, chap. XVII, esp. p. 330, and Bentham's *An Essay on Political Tactics*, 1816.

22 Joseph Redlich, *The Procedure of the House of Commons* (trs. A. E. Steinthal), 1908, a masterly historical treatment showing the interaction between parliamentary procedure and governmental structure and functioning.

23 Cf. note 7 above.

24 Bertrand de Jouvenel, in his *The Pure Theory of Politics*, 1963, has drawn attention, in chap. 3 of Part VI, to the significance of manners in politics, esp. pp. 193 ff. The almost complete lack of manners among the radical youth of our day is one of the most disconcerting features of their activities and verbal expressions. In Germany, never a country distinguished by good manners, in politics, love, or anything else, these elements have descended into the gutter.

2/Traditionalist Theory

1 Werner Jaeger, *Paideia: The Ideas of Greek Culture*, 1939, I, esp. Book I, chap. VIII, pp. 137–47; Jaeger does not give primary attention to *nomos*.

2 Felix Heinimann, *Nomos und Physis*, 1946, p. 89.

3 *The Digest*, I, 3, 2, quoting the great Chrysippus.

4 Hannah Arendt, *Fragwürdige Traditionsbestände im politischen Denken der Gegenwart*, p. 23, asserts this insight, but exaggerates it; in the English version *Between Past and Future*, 1961, the statement occurs on p. 25.

5 Cf. R. Sohm, *The Institutions of Roman Law*, 1892; the literature on the development of Roman law is, of course, vast; as relevant to our problem, I would mention Fritz Schulz, *History of Roman Legal Science*, 1946; James Muirhead, *Historical Introduction to the Private Law of Rome*, 1886; Paul Krüger, *Geschichte der Quellen und Literatur des Römischen Rechts*, 1888; R. von Ihering, *Der Geist des Römischen Rechts*, 1866–71.

6 The Chinese Emperor Shi Huang Ti is discussed in this perspective by Chinese and Western scholarship. Cf. Kenneth Scott Latourette, *The Chinese—Their History and Culture*, 2nd edn, 1942, pp. 91–100; and more especially John K. Fairbank (ed.), *Chinese Thought and Institutions*, 1957, p. 817.

7 E. F. Bruck, *Über römisches Recht im Rahmen der Kulturgeschichte*, 1954, has learnedly developed this point; for Polybius' text see Polybius, *The Histories*, Book VI, chap. 4 (trs. Paton, Loeb Classics, Vol. III, 1966).

8 Nicolo Machiavelli, *The Discourses*, Book I, chap. 18.

9 For further detail, see my *Philosophy of Law in Historical Perspective*, 2nd edn, 1963, chaps. IX and X.

10 Edward Coke, *Reports*, XII, pp. 64–5.

11 The doctrine of the artificial reason of the law is further discussed by Roscoe Pound, *An Introduction to the Philosophy of Law*, 1922; cf. also his *The Spirit of the Common Law*, 1921.

12 On the prerogative cf. my op. cit. (note 9), pp. 80 ff

13 Louis I. Bredvold and Ralph G. Ross, *The Philosophy of Edmund Burke*, 1960, chaps. VI and VII; the quote is found at p. 156. Other quotations from Burke, unless otherwise noted, are also found in this volume. A recent study of Burke deserves mention here, although it does not concern itself specifically with tradition, Francis Canavan, *The Political Reason of Edmund Burke*, 1960. In his analysis of prescription, pp. 120 ff., the author shows that for Burke reason and tradition are not antithetical, but mutually reinforcing; there is a reasonable presumption in favor of the established order of things.

14 Edmund Burke, *Works*, in nine vols. is the edition from which I cite; published in the United States in 1839, its vol. III contains Burke's *Reflexions on the Revolution in France* (1790); for the quotation in the text see p. 452. Ibid. p. 179, Burke says: 'If prescription be once shaken, no species of property is secure . . .' However, prescription does not constitute an absolute title. For the same reason Burke also said that 'there is a time when the hoary head of inveterate abuse will neither draw reverence, nor obtain protection'. The point is forcefully made by Canavan, op. cit. p. 122.

15 The general problem of restoration was recently explored in a comparative study by Robert A. Kann, *The Problem of Restoration*, 1968. In Chapter III he treats tradition at length, and he comments that 'if there ever was an official state philosophy of the restoration in a literally narrow sense, it would be that of Bonald and De Maistre . . . They shared a hatred of the revolution, a denial of the persuasiveness of human reason, a belief in the basic inequality of men, and a negative view of human character . . .', p. 344.

16 Peter Richard Rohden, in his study *Joseph de Maistre als Politischer Theoretiker, Ein Beitrag . . .*, 1929, cites on this a letter from de Maistre's *Oeuvres*, IX, p. 11; it was to Costa de Beauregard.

17 *Considérations sur la France*, new edn, 1845 (Lyon), p. 141; cf. also chaps. VIII and II.

18 Ibid., p. 9 (chap. II).

19 De Maistre, *Examen de la Philosophie de Bacon*, p. 457. Striking comments have been made by Walter Benjamin on the 'destructive character' in his *Schriften*, ed. Adorno, 1955, Vol. II, pp. 1–3. 'The destructive character knows only one maxim: to make room, and only one activity: to move out . . . . The destructive character does not recognize anything lasting . . . he transforms everything into ruins, not for the sake of the ruins, but for the sake of the road through them.'

20 Rohden, op. cit., p. 147.

21 De Maistre, *Du Pape*, Book I, chap. XX, p. 157, in the new edition of 1843 (Paris): it reads: 'La fraternité qui résulte d'une langue commune est un lien mystérieux d'une force immense.' De Maistre is speaking here of Latin in the Church.

22 De Maistre, *Soirées de Saint Pétersbourg*, Entretien I; cf. also chap. VII.

23 On Montesquieu whose *Oeuvres Complètes* of 1835 I use, cf. *Esprit des Lois*, 1748, Book XI, but not solely the famous chap. VI about Britain, but also the discussion of Rome and more esp. chap. VII, p. 270.

24 Bonald's work on power, both political and ecclesiastical (religious), *Oeuvres*, Vols. XIII–XV.

25 On Bonald's traditionalism and how it is related to his sociological notions, Robert Spaemann has recently published a very interesting study entitled *Der Ursprung der Soziologie aus dem Geist der Restauration—Studien über L.G.A. de Bonald*, 1959 (Muenchen). Spämann rightly considers the theory of language the key point of 'traditionalism', pp. 46–62.

3/Tradition and the Science of Politics

1 The notion of 'negative revolution' was first developed by me in an article 'The Political Theory of the New Democratic Constitutions', in *Constitutions and Constitutional Trends Since World War II*, edited by Arnold Zurcher, 1951, 1955. For a more recent statement cf. my *Constitutional Government and Democracy*, 4th edn, 1968, pp. 151 ff.

2 Cf. e.g. the volume of *Annales de la Philosophie Politique*, dedicated to this topic, and the literature cited there, and my *Man and His Government*, where political ideology is discussed in chap. 4, entitled 'The Function of Ideas and Ideology'. I define 'ideologies' as 'action-related systems of ideas'. They typically contain a program and their essential function is to unite organizations that are built around them.

3 Max Weber, *Wirtschaft und Gesellschaft*, 2nd edn, 1925, I, para. 7. The translation is my own, since I cannot accept Parsons' widely followed translation, especially the rendering of certain key terms, such as *Herrschaft* which is, in my opinion, rule.

4 On foundation and foundation myth, cf. my work, cited above, note 2, chap. 22 entitled 'The Founding of a Political Order' and chap. 5 entitled 'The Political Myth', esp. pp. 101 ff.

5 Cf. chap. VIII in my *Totalitarian Dictatorship and Autocracy*, 2nd edn, 1965, which deals with the roots of ideology, and my contribution to *Totalitarianism in Perspective: Three Views*, 1969, pp. 130 ff.

6 Unfortunately, quotable material has not yet become available. Cf. R. Tugwell, in 1970, drafted a new constitution for a United Republics of America, and Archibald McLeish published an article in the *Saturday Review* (of Literature), August 29, 1970, called 'The Festival of Freedom' which responded to a proposal made by the Commission on the Bicentennial of the American Revolution. McLeish's key point is that 'the Bicentennial should be framed in action, not a backward looking self-congratulation on a past we have ourselves betrayed, but a new beginning . . .' Cf. also the publication of the American Assembly, *The Forty-Eight States: Their Tasks as Policy-Makers and Administrators*, 1955, for the federal aspect of these discussions.

7 Robert E. Lane, *Political Ideology*, 1962; he defines his understanding of ideology on pp. 14–15; it is broader than mine, but includes the programmatic, action-related aspect.

8 Besides the references in notes 2, 5 and 7, let me insist that I do not believe there is an 'end of ideology' in sight, as Daniel Bell, following Raymond Aron, has argued in his *The End of Ideology*, 1960. Cf. also my work, as cited in note 5, esp. at pp. 85 ff.

9 Gabriel A. Almond and Sidney Verba, *The Civic Culture—Political Attitudes and Democracy in Five Nations*, 1963; I cite the paperback edition, published by Little, Brown & Co., 1965.

10 Ibid., p. 5.

11 Ibid., p. 13.

12 Ibid., p. 12.

13 From among the numerous studies, let me cite Alex Inkeles and Daniel Levinson, 'National Character: The Study of Modal Personality and Socio-Cultural Systems', in Gardner Lindzey, (ed.) *Handbook of Social Psychology*, Cambridge, Mass., 1954, Vol. II; Margaret Mead, 'The Study of National Character', in Daniel Lerner and Harold D. Lasswell, *The Policy Sciences*, Stanford, 1951, and Alex Inkeles, 'National Character and Modern Political Systems', in Frank L. K. Hsu (ed.), *Psychological Anthropology*, Homewood, Ill., 1961. Lucian W. Pye's *Politics, Personality, and Nation Building*, New Haven, 1962, approaches the problem in collective terms, and with reference to a non-European culture.

14 Salvador de Madariaga's *Portrait of Europe*, 1950, is a striking illustration of this kind of purely speculative and indeed poetic approach—refreshing in a sense, because for him, a Spaniard, Spanish national character emerges with the most laudatory adjectives.

15 See the material notes in notes 13.

16 Lucius D. Clay, *Decision in Germany*, 1950, p. 436.

17 See my article 'Rebuilding the German Constitution', in *American Political Science Review*, Vol. XLIII, 1949, p. 462.

18 Lloyd I. Rudolph and Suzanne Hoeber Rudolph, *The Modernity of Tradition—Political Development in India*, 1967.

19 Ibid., p. 3; in a footnote the authors formulate 'heuristically useful contrasts' of modernity and tradition as follows: 'modernity assumes that local ties and parochial perspectives give way to universal commitments and cosmopolitan attitudes; that the truths of utility, calculation, and science take precedence over those of the emotions, the sacred, and the non-rational; that the individual rather than the group be the primary unit of society and politics; that the associations in which men live and work be based on choice not birth; that mastery rather than fatalism orient their attitude toward the material and human environment; that identity be chosen and achieved, not ascribed and affirmed; that work be separated from family, residence, and community in bureaucratic organizations . . .' and so forth. It is evident that these contrasts are moulded in their specificity by the authors' concern over Indian and European tradition, and that modernity, as seen by them, is itself a particular tradition, but they serve to illustrate the interrelationship of the two very well.

20 Ibid., pp. 216-19, 247-9.

21 Ibid., p. 14.

22 Hannah Arendt, *Between Past and Future*, 1961, p. 17.

23 Ibid., p. 21.

24 Characteristically, Plato's guardians must return to the city and cannot remain in the contemplation of the world of ideas outside the cave. In the *Republic*, 499, Plato (Socrates) explicitly states his conviction thus: 'it is quite *unreasonable* to suppose that it cannot be realized. The constitution we have described has arisen, exists and will arise when the muse of philosophy becomes mistress of a city. That she should do so is not impossible. Nor are the things we have described impossible.' In agreement with me is D. Greene, *Man in His Pride*, chaps. IX–XIII. The matter is discussed briefly in my *Introduction to Political Theory*, chap. 6, in the context of Plato's idea of justice and the role of the political élite. For the *Seventh Letter* see Kurt von Fritz, *Platon in Sizilien und das Problem der Philosophenherrschaft*, 1968, esp. chap. I. Wisely, Edith Hamilton and Huntington Cairns included it in their edition of *Plato, Collected Dialogues*, Bollinger Foundation, LXXI (no date), pp. 157 ff.

25 Carl Friedrich von Weizsaecker, 'Die Rolle der Tradition in der Philosophie', in *Hundert Jahre Philosophische Bibliothek, 1868–1968*, 1968, pp. 27–42.

26 Albert Somit and Joseph Tanenhaus, *The Development of American Political Science—From Burgess to Behaviorism*, 1967.

27 The reason I put 'materialist' into quotation marks is that Marx lays stress on the primary role of the control of the means of production which is, strictly speaking, not a material, but a social phenomenon. This was stressed by Joseph Schumpeter, *Capitalism, Socialism and Democracy*, 1942, pp. 10 ff.

28 In the heat of the Second World War, I tried to restate democratic theory in *The New Belief in the Common Man*, 1942. It was one of many such efforts, e.g. A. D. Lindsay, *The Modern Democratic State*, 1943; Carl L. Becker, *Modern Democracy*, 1941; Neal Riemer, *The Democratic Experiment: American Political Theory*, I, 1967, and two surveys, William F. Russell and Thomas H. Briggs, *The Meaning of Democracy*, 1941 and John R. Beery, *Current Conceptions of Democracy*, 1943. The clash between Western and Soviet notions of democracy has preoccupied the discusions since the end of the Second World War, and the United Nations, through U N E S C O, undertook, but failed, to compromise the issue; see for a recent Soviet view Viktor M. Tchikvadze, *Gosudarstvo demokratia Zakonosti*, 1967. A good recent statement is found in Harvey Wheeler, *Democracy in a Revolutionary Era—The Political Order of Today*, 1968. I commented on Tchikvadze's discussion by remarking that 'a totalitarian dictatorship can also be described as a "perfect democracy" in the sense that the people, represented by the party, which in turn is represented by its leaders, exercise total and unrestrained power'. See my contribution to *Totalitarianism in Perspective*, 1969, p. 136.

29 Notably Reinhold Niebuhr in several works, e.g. *Christianity and Power Politics*, 1940, *Moral Man and Immoral Society: A Study in Ethics and Politics*, 1932, and *The Nature and Destiny of Man: A Christian Interpretation*, 1941.

30 The most impressive restatement of this conception in recent years was made by Karl Jaspers (and Kurt Rossmann), *Die Idee der Universität*, 1961.

4/The Rational Ground of Authority

1 Earlier formulations of the position developed in this and the following chapters include a chapter in my *Man and His Government*, 1963, and my contribution, entitled 'Authority, Reason and Discretion' in *Nomos*, I (ed. Friedrich), 1958, *Authority*, pp. 28 ff. where references to earlier articles are made. Recently, Chaim Perelman has taken a very similar line in his lecture 'Autorité, Idéologie et Violence', published in *Le Champ de l'Argumentation*, 1970 (Brussels). Note also the work by Arendt, de Jouvenel and others referred to below. A striking case of the contrast between formal power and authority is found in Norman Mailer's *The Naked and the Dead*. The tension between Lieutenant Hearn and Sergeant Croft is basically that between the holder of formal authority, Lt Hearn, and the man with genuine authority, Sgt Croft. Croft, the men all realize, 'knows' the problems of jungle warfare. And Hearn realizes it too. 'If he wasn't careful, Croft would keep effective command of the platoon. The trouble was that Croft knew more, and it was silly to disagree with him . . .', p. 358

2 On Bonald and de Maistre cf. above, Chapter 2.

3   E.g. Harold D. Lasswell and A. Kaplan, *Power and Society*, 1950, esp. pp. 133 ff.

4   See Theodor Mommsen, *Römisches Staatsrecht* (2nd edn, 1888), Vol. III, pp. 1033 ff. I should like to call attention in this connection to the fact that Apollo was believed to be the 'augmenter'. He was the God of the Sun, of reason and moderation, cf. W. K. C. Guthrie, *The Greeks and their Gods*, 1950, pp. 183 ff. Guthrie wrote of 'Apollo's primary aspect, his championship of law and order . . . limit, moderation, obedience to authority, and condemning excess in all its forms.' (p. 203).

5   This derivation has been authoritatively questioned by R. Heinze in his article 'Auctoritas' in *Hermes*, Vol. IX, 1925, pp. 348–66.

6   Chaim Perelman, *The New Rhetoric*, 1969 (a translation of the original *La Nouvelle Rhétorique*—with L. Obrechts-Tytega, 1958), does not consider the problem of authority, in spite of its central importance for all rhetoric (and propaganda). Cf. in this connection Michael Polanyi, *Personal Knowledge*, 1958, pp. 207 ff., 374 ff. and *passim* where the role of authority in science is considered.

7   Chaim Perelman in the work, cited above, note 1, esp. pp. 207 ff.

8   Aristotle, *Rhetorics*, I, 2. We cannot here explore this important work, but let me say that Aristotle's concern with the emotions and the character of the speaker shows that he was aware of the problems of authority in rhetorics.

9   Thomas Hobbes, *Leviathan*, 1651, chap. X; Rousseau, *Contrat Social*, 1761, Book II. For Hobbes the key to authority is 'the right of doing any act', right and power being for Hobbes virtually synonymous, as they were for Spinoza who blandly stated that 'the big fish devour the little fish by natural right'—Spinoza, *A Theologico-Political Treatise*, 1670, chap. XVI— a view which had great appeal to Napoleon and Bismarck, as it had to the absolute monarchs of Spinoza's own time.

10   Sir Edward Coke, *Reports*, 65; cf. also my *Philosophy of Law in Historical Perspective*, 1958 and 1963, chap. 10.

11   Thomas D. Wheldon, *The Vocabulary of Politics*, 1953, pp. 50–56. Cf. also P. H. Nowell Smith *et al.*, 'Politics, Psychology and Art', in Aristotelian Society, *Symposium: Science and Politics*, Supplement of their *Proceedings*, Vol. 33, 1949.

12   Max Weber, *Wirtschaft und Gesellschaft*, 2nd edn, 1925, pp. 16–20 and *passim* equates authority with legitimacy, as do many others, and thereby misses the key aspect of authority, namely its relation to reason. That same mistake is not made by Herbert Spiro, 'Authority, Values, and Policy', in *Nomos*, I (ed. Friedrich), pp. 49 ff.

13   Cf. chap. IX on power and leadership in my work cited above, note 1.

14   Michael Polanyi has developed this interesting notion in *The Tacit Dimension*, 1966.

15   Plato, *The Laws*, 723.

16   As is done by Perelman in the article cited above, note 1.

17   Cf. Donald G. Morgan, *Congress and the Constitution*, 1966.

18   Bertrand de Jouvenel, *Sovereignty*, 1957, chap. 2, esp. pp. 28–31; cf. also his article in *Nomos*, I (ed. Friedrich), 1958, 'Authority: The Efficient Imperative', pp. 160 ff. In the latter article, de Jouvenel argued that authority is the efficient imperative—a kind of communication; hence he leans toward my view that authority is basically a quality of communications.

19   George C. Lewis, *An Essay on the Influence of Authority*, 1849; Lewis was a Utilitarian.

20   See Chap. 9 below.

21 H. Arendt in *The Origins of Totalitarianism*, 1951, at end. Her views are adopted by Henry S. Kariel, in his concluding essay 'Foundations for Politics' in his *In Search of Authority: Twentieth-Century Political Thought*, 1964, p. 246. This collection of approaches to authority in recent years is valuable, though incomplete.

5/The Genesis of Authority: Value

1 Herbert Spiro, 'Authority, Values, and Policy', in *Nomos*, I, 1958, p. 54.
2 Ibid.
3 Norman Jacobson, 'Knowledge, Tradition, and Authority, A Note on the American Experience', in *Nomos*, Vol. I, pp. 123 ff.
4 Chaim Perelman, 'Autorité, Idéologie, et Violence', in *Le Champ de l'Argumentation*, 1970, pp. 209 ff.; Spiro, article cited in note 1; my article in *Nomos*, I, etc.
5 The term 'socialization' which has come into wide use is subject to serious objections which will be found in my *Man and His Government*, 1963, pp. 620 ff. See also Gabriel A. Almond and James S. Coleman, *The Politics of Developing Areas*, 1957 which is bassd on Herbert Hyman, *Political Socialization*, 1959, p. 18, where the term is used as a general substitute for education.
6 If, on the other hand, the power of the parents is wielded without such growing participation and insight on the part of the young person, then coercive relations develop which, devoid of authority, lead to the destruction of the family or to the destruction of the personality, depending on vitality and other factors. This thought is the sound core of 'progressive' education which has however gone beyond this; cf. my 'This Progressive Education', *Atlantic Monthly*, 1934, pp. 421 ff.
7 On founding cf. besides my work cited above in note 5, chap. 22, Bertrand de Jouvenel, *De la Souveraineté*, 1955, pp. 50 ff. Cf. also his article in *Nomos*, I, pp. 159 ff.
8 Cf. the study by Yves Tavernier and Hélène Delorme, *Les Paysans Français et l'Unité Européenne*, 1969, pp. 123 ff.
9 Hannah Arendt in her article 'What was Authority?' in *Nomos*, I, pp. 81 ff. She begins with the sentence, 'It is my contention that authority has vanished from the modern world . . .', reasons for which she offered in 'Authority in the Twentieth Century', *Review of Politics*, 1956.
10 Rousseau, *Contrat Social*, Book II, chap. 12.
11 The German phrase is 'ruhender Pol in der Erscheinungen Flucht'.
12 The contrast between a 'command ethic' and a 'value ethic' was worked out by Herbert Spiegelberg in his seminal work *Gesetz und Sittengesetz*, 1935. It is built in part upon Max Scheler's celebrated *Der Formalismus in der Ethik und die materiale Wertethik*, 2. edn 1926.
13 Jefferson, besides his well-known letter on the tree of liberty that must be fertilized every so often by the blood of revolutionaries, in his First Inaugural, uttered the noble sentiment: 'If there be any among us who would wish to dissolve this Union or to change its republican form, let them stand undisturbed as monuments of the safety with which error of opinion may be tolerated where reason is left free to combat it.' See *Writings*, 1859, Vol. III. Is reason thus free in a world of totalitarians? Abraham Lincoln, in speaking on the Mexican War, said in Congress on January 12, 1848, 'Any people anywhere being inclined and having the power, have the right to rise up and shake off the existing government, and form a new one that suits

them better. This is a most valuable, a most sacred right . . .', and he added,
'It is a quality of revolutions not to go by old ideas or old laws . . .' Cf.
Complete Works, ed. Nicolay and Haym, 2nd edn, 1905, Vol. I, pp. 338 ff.
14 Jacobson, op. cit. (note 3 above), pp. 123 ff.
15 My work, cited above note 5, chap. II, esp. pp. 53 ff.
16 For the economist's position, see O. H. Taylor, *A History of Economic
Thought*, 1960, pp. 101 ff., 188 ff., 244 ff., 264 ff., 325 ff., 450 ff. Economists
have traditionally called instrumental values either 'market value' or
'exchange value'. A great painting may have an inherent value of beauty,
and an exchange value varying with time and circumstances.
17 Preoccupation with instrumental values leads to value relativism, while
over-concern with inherent values occasions value dogmatism or absolutism.
Political science needs to avoid either of these extremes, and to elucidate
inherent value, while exploring instrumental value.
18 Hobbes explicitly rejected the notion of a 'highest Good' (*summum bonum*),
but implicitly argued it is contained in the 'first law of nature'. There have
been conflicting notions on this in recent work. Arnold Brecht, in his
Political Theory, chap. VIII, reviewed these, but concluded that no one 'has
been able to "prove" scientifically that his particular answer is right. The
evidence leads to the conclusion that no rank or hierarchy of values exists as
a universal preference of politically organized men; they fail to make up
their mind'.
19 Cf. on this my *Transcendant Justice*, 1964, chap. V, esp. at pp. 110 ff.
20 In the face of an executive and a legislature who were reluctant to deal with
racial discrimination, the U.S. Supreme Court has, since 1954, and in a
number of dramatic decisions, beginning with *Brown v. Board of Education*,
347 U.S. 483, undertaken to remind the American people and its government that the egalitarian principles of the constitution were being neglected
and called for stricter enforcement. See for this, Arthur E. Sutherland,
Constitutionalism in America, 1965, chap. 17, esp. pp. 536 ff.

6/Authority and Discretion

1 John Locke, *Two Treatises on Government*, 1690. Second Treatise, para. 160.
2 Ibid., para. 159.
3 A. V. Dicey, *Law of the Constitution*, 8th edn, 1926, p. 420. Concerning
Dicey's ideological position, I wrote a critical evaluation for the *Festschrift*
of G. Leibholz, *Die Moderne Demokratie und Ihr Recht*, 1966, under the
title 'Englische Verfassungsideologie im neunzehnten Jahrhundert', 1966.
4 James I developed these ideas in his *The Law of Free Monarchies*, which can
be found in Charles H. McIlwain, *The Political Works of James I*, 1918; note
especially McIlwain's introduction for illuminating comment.
5 Cf. my *Philosophy of Law in Historical Perspective*, 2nd edn, 1963, chap. X.
6 Ivor Jennings, *Cabinet Government*, 1936, chap. XII.
7 There is an interesting parallel between Locke's view and the Chinese
tradition of 'tsung-tung' which has been rendered as 'legitimate authority';
it teaches that no authority can be legitimate which fails to fulfil the function for which it was created in serving the public good. Cf. below Chap. 8.
8 This way of 'defining' discretion emerged for me from discussions with
colleagues of the Harvard Law School in a group organized by Lon Fuller
in 1955–57. No published record exists.
9 We face here the problem of general clauses which have been abused so

much in autocratic regimes. A German jurist, J. W. Hedemann, stressed the dangers of such a flight into general clauses in German judicial decisions preceding Hitler's advent to power in *Die Flucht in die Generalklauseln*, 1933.

10 Very interesting on the general problem is Fritz von Hippel, *Die Perversion von Rechtsordnungen*, 1955, who gives many concrete illustrations of how such general clauses (and some not so general!) may be carried beyond the limits allowed by the system. As for the matter of discretion, they constitute cases of the *abuse* of discretion.

11 Karl Llewellyn, *Jurisprudence: Realism in Theory and Practice*, 1962; he gives many references.

12 Lucius D. Clay, *Decision in Germany*, 1950, pp. 123 ff. Robert D. Murphy, *Diplomat Among Warriors*, 1964, pp. 290–92, is rather evasive on the issue, but the very stress he lays on his personal good relations with Clay betray the problem; cf. esp. pp. 291–2.

13 J. Todd, in his dissertation 'The Debate on United States Reparation Policy After World War II', Harvard University Dissertation, 1970, has been able to elucidate at least part of this difficult story.

14 Murphy, op. cit. (note 12).

15 In my *Foreign Policy in the Making*, 1938, I gave many illustrations; cf. also H. Bradford Westerfield, *Foreign Policy and Party Politics*, 1955, a mine of information on this issue in America. For Germany see Hans W. Baade, *Das Verhältnis von Parlament und Regierung im Bereich der Auswertigen Gewalt der Bundesrepublik Deutschland*, 1962.

16 Such tightening up is now being widely discussed in America. Thus the provision on declaration of war could be implemented by one which would outlaw the deployment of American forces abroad, or at least drafted soldiers, in military combat abroad without such a formal declaration of war; likewise executive agreements and similar commitments could be included in the provision requiring senatorial assent.

17 The Committee on Foreign Affairs or the Senate and the House could be exempted from the seniority rule by making them subject to an explicit electoral choice.

18 My *Foreign Policy in the Making*, 1938, chap. 3; the issue has since been treated by writers on foreign policy. Cf. e.g. Kenneth N. Waltz, *Foreign Policy and Democratic Politics*, 1967 and J. N. Rosenau and others in R. Barry Farrell (ed.), *Approaches to Comparative and International Politics*, 1966, pp. 27 ff.

19 The Brookings Institution, Washington, D.C., *Major Problems of United States Foreign Policy*, *1949–1950*, 1949.

20 Ibid., p. 21; such phrases recur in ambassadorial instructions of the eighteenth century.

21 Ibid., p. 30.

22 Ibid., pp. 34 ff.

23 In an article in *Aussenpolitik*, Vol. I, 1950 'Das Ende der Kabinettspolitik', pp. 20 ff., I sketched this development. Cf. also Gabriel Almond, *The American People and Foreign Policy*, 1950, 1960, and Westerfield, cited in note 15 above.

24 Chester I. Bernard, in *The Functions of the Executive*, 1956, pp. 161 ff. makes this point emphatically in his theory of authority. These pages are reprinted in Shankar A. Yelaja, *Authority and Social Work*, Toronto, 1971. Barnard develops there his notion of objective authority for which cf. above, Chap. 4.

7/Freedom versus Authority

1 John Stuart Mill, *On Liberty*, The Liberal Arts Press, New York, 1956 (original edition 1859), pp. 3 and 4. The editor, Currin Shields, in his preface, does not make the point. See for the range of isuses raised by Mill's essay, *Nomos*, Vol. IV, on 'Liberty', 1962.

2 'As far as the opinions, beliefs and values involved in such reasoned elaboration, that is, in such argumentation, are concerned, they may be one or many, readily identifiable or highly speculative and abstract. One value, such as truth or justice or health, may predominate, or they may be an infinitely complex array of values, such as are represented by a culture or way of life.' Cited from my *Man and His Government*, pp. 224–5. What matters is that such opinions provide a reference frame for reasoned elaboration.

3 This stress on subjectivity is found in a number of contributors to the volume edited by Shankar A. Yelaja, *Authority and Social Work—Concept and Use*, Toronto, 1971, notably Chester I. Barnard, 'The Theory of Authority', who makes 'acceptance' a key criterion of authoritative communications, pp. 49 ff.; and the editor himself who states that 'Authority and freedom are in the final analysis subjective notions . . .' in his 'Freedom and Authority' at p. 41. This tendency is traceable to Max Weber whose key passages are reproduced in this volume, pp. 65 ff. under the title 'The Type of Authority' Weber's position is more fully discussed below, Chap. 8 in connection with legitimacy, which Weber confuses with authority.

4 On truth and justice in politics, see my work cited above, note 2, chap. 14.

5 The passage cited from Barnard, above note 3, reads more fully 'Authority is the character of a communication (order in a formal organization) by virtue of which it is accepted by a contributor to or "member" of the organization as governing the action he contributes'. I agree that ultimately authority is a quality of communications, at least in an objective sense, but do not believe that it is sound to make acceptance crucial, on account of the difficulty of coping with false authority as shown in the text.

6 The German original (by Goethe) reads: 'Erst in der Beschränkung zeigt sich der Meister . . .'

7 See my work cited in note 2, chaps. 20 and 21, where freedom (liberty) is more fully discussed, and extensive references to the literature are found, notably to Adler, Oppenheim, and others.

8 This is the classical position of Locke and Kant; Yelaja cites Kenneth Pray as of the opinion that 'there is no absolute freedom in this world', op. cit. (note 3), p. 41. The position is also central to Isaiah Berlin's *Four Essays on Liberty*, 1969, esp. his inaugural, 'Two Concepts of Liberty', pp. 118 ff., first published in 1958; there are those who 'believe in liberty in the "positive"—self-directive—sense', and there are those others who want authority placed in their own hands (freedom of participation!), whereas the first kind want 'to curb authority as such'.

9 My work, cited in note 2, chaps. 9 and 10, dealing with power and rule.

10 Such excess of freedom will not be recognized by those who assume, contrary to evidence, that humans wish a maximum of freedom, and 'the more freedom the better'. Neither of these are true, and in politics it is not possible to maximize all three dimensions of freedom, as is shown in the citation, note 7.

11 In view of the large literature on this issue, I shall here refer the reader to a broadly conceived introduction with many viewpoints, to be found in *Daedalus*, Winter 1968, esp. the opening paper by Martin Seymour Lipset, 'Students and Politics in Comparative Perspective', pp. 1–20.

12 In the work cited above, note 2, I defined the free as follows (p. 353): 'when and to the extent that human beings, either individually or collectively, act politically—that is, opine, prefer, decide questions of policy, for example— without the interference of other human beings, they shall be called free'. The present further reflections on freedom and authority make me feel that this definition must be further sharpened by adding the qualification, after 'interference of other human beings', 'except when based on genuine authority'. For such authority-based interference is not only compatible with freedom, but an essential condition of it.

13 See the issue of *Daedalus*, Winter 1970, entitled 'The Embattled University', and including contributions from Erik Erikson, Clark Kerr and others. Compare also the magisterial study by Christopher Jenks and David Riesman, *The Academic Revolution in America*, 1970.

14 John Stuart Mill, op. cit. (note 1), chap. IV, pp. 91 ff.

15 Ibid., p. 95.

16 The matter is discussed in my (with Z. Brzezinski) *Totalitarian Dictatorship and Autocracy*, 2nd edn, 1965, chap. 6 (on succession), pp. 77 ff.

8/Authority and Legitimacy

1 Max Weber, *Wirtschaft und Gesellschaft*, 1922, 2nd edn, 1925, pp. 16–20, equates authority with legitimacy, or seems to do so; the text is not clear. Cf. chap. 13 of my *Man and His Government*, 1963.

2 Weber, op. cit.

3 Ibid., p. 172, and the discussion in my (with Z. Brzezinski) *Totalitarian Dictatorship and Autocracy*, rev. edn, 1965, pp. 41 ff.

4 Weber, op. cit. In my *Man and His Government* I developed a distinction between several kinds of leadership, that of the initiator, the conservator, and the protector. As these are differentiated, charismatic leadership partakes of the differentiation, and thus charisma is affected by it. The notion of routine is more nearly applicable to conservator and protector than to initiator.

5 I first developed this point in 'Political Leadership and the Problem of Charismatic Power', *The Journal of Politics*, Vol. 23, 1961, pp. 3 ff.

6 See my contribution to *Totalitarianism in Perspective: Three Views*, 1969, pp. 123 ff. There I said: 'Presumably the most striking change in the theory and practice of totalitarian regimes appears to be the development of a substantial consensus in the Soviet Union. To be sure the existence of such a consensus is difficult to prove . . . Even so, what evidence we do have . . . all points so uniformly to such a conclusion that we are justified in assuming a consensus to exist . . .' This question leads to the problem of ideology. Ideologies are dynamic entities, and their changes show their vitality. Cf. ibid., pp. 136 ff.

7 Dolf Sternberger in a good article in the *International Encyclopedia of the Social Sciences*, Vol. IX, pp. 244 ff. developed this distinction without stressing what the two kinds of legitimacy have in common when he wrote that 'legitimacy is the foundation of such governmental power as is exercised both with a consciousness on the government's part that it has a right to govern and with some recognition by the governed of that right'. I believe the latter to be crucial.

8 Carl Schmitt, *Legalität und Legitimität*, 1932, discussed by Sternberger, op. cit. (note 7).

9 See my *Philosophy of Law in Historical Perspective*, 2nd edn, 1963, chap. IV, at p. 30, and chap. V, at pp. 39–40.

10 Such a statement presupposes that there prevails a 'belief in law' as it does in Western nations under the Judaeo-Christian tradition. For a striking illustration of this root of the belief, cf. the *Letter to the Galatians*, chap. 3, esp. verses 10–12, 19–21.

11 An interesting recent analysis is found in Klaus von Beyme, *Die Politische Elite in der Bundesrepublik Deutschland*, 1970.

12 On ideology, cf. op. cit., above note 6, and chap. 4 of Friedrich, op. cit., note 1.

13 Robert E. Lane, *Political Ideology—Why the American Common Man Believes What he Does*, 1962; Lane does not clarify what is to be understood by 'common man', for which see my *The New Belief in the Common Man*, 1942 (rev. edn, 1950). Cf. for a broad review of prevailing ideologies *Ideologies and Modern Politics*, Reo M. Christenson and others, 1971.

14 Jerome Bruner, *Mandate from the People*, 1944, is more concerned with opinions about issues than about persons, but see pp. 159 and 175. Very valuable, Bernard Rubin, *Political Television*, 1967, esp. chaps. 2, 4, and 6 (on Kennedy and Johnson); also Charles A. H. Thomson, *Television and Presidential Politics*, 1956 (on Eisenhower). A special issue arose in connection with the television debates between Kennedy and Nixon in 1960, on which see Sidney Kraus (ed.), *The Great Debates—Background, Perspectives, Effects*, 1962 and Karl Maxo and others, 'The Great Debates', An Occasional Paper—Center for the Study of Democratic Institutions (ed. H. S. Ashmore), 1962. See also the American Political Science Association's *Report of the Commission on Presidential Debates*, 1964. The text of the debates was published in Senate, 87th Congress, *Freedom of Communications*, Final Report, Part III, December 11, 1961.

15 Arthur M. Schlesinger, *The Age of Roosevelt—The Crisis of the Old Order, 1933–1937*, 1957 and James MacGregor Burns, *Roosevelt—The Soldier of Freedom, 1940–1945*, 1970, and *Roosevelt—The Lion and the Fox*, 1956.

16 See the editorials of Marion Gräfin Dönhoff, in *Die Zeit*, 1967.

17 For example, this is done by Thomas D. Wheldon, *The Vocabulary of Politics*, pp. 50–56; he does not use the term 'legitimacy', but speaks of 'the general approval' of the governed.

9/The Anarchist Challenge

1 George Woodcock, *Anarchism—A History of Libertarian Ideas and Movements*, 1962, p. 9. This valuable over-all treatment suffers from the confusion indicated in the subtitle. (See chap. 7 on the problem of liberty and authority.) Also very interesting among recent comparative studies of anarchism is James Joll's *The Anarchists*, 1964, and Rudolf Krämer-Badoni, *Anarchismus: Geschichte und Gegenwart einer Utopie*, 1970, which is distinguished by its repeated discussions of the parallels with contemporary anarchism. The latter is also the subject of a collection of essays edited by Erwin K. Scheuch, *Die Wiedertäufer der Wohlstandsgesellschaft—Eine kritische Untersuchung der 'Neuen Linken' und ihrer Dogmen*, 1968.

2 Proudhon, in his famous *Qu'est-ce la Propriété?* at one point tells his readers: 'Je ne suis pas un agent de discorde, ni un défenseur de la sédition. Je prévois l'histoire par quelques jours; je dévoile la vérité . . .' He considers himself basically a truth-seeker.

3 I have dealt with this anarchist controversy over violence in a paper by that title read at the annual meeting of the Institut de la Philosophie Politique at Colmar, July 3, 1971, and to be published in the Institut's *Annales de la Philosophie Politique* in 1972.

4 See Andrew Hacker's article in the *International Encyclopedia of the Social Sciences*, 1968, Vol. I, pp. 284 ff.

5 Gertrude Himmelfarb's selection: *Essays on Freedom and Power by John Emerich Edward Dalberg-Acton*, 1948, p. 184. The essay is entitled 'Nationality'.

6 Alexis de Tocqueville, *Democracy in America*, did not stress this, however.

7 Cf. my *Political Pathology*, 1971; a chapter on violence contains a discussion of the vigilantes and cites additional literature.

8 The published translation of Max Stirner's work bears the title *The Ego and His Own*, 1963, which fails to convey the solipsistic emphasis of this extraordinary work, *Der Einzige und sein Eigentum*, 2nd edn, 1882.

9 Arthur Bauer, *Essai sur les Révolutions*, 1908, p. 11: 'les révolutions sont les changements tentés ou réalisés par la force dans la constitution des sociétés'.

10 William Godwin, *Political Justice*, Book VII, chap. II, p. 162; this chapter discusses 'the general disadvantages of coercion'.

11 Ibid., p. 165.

12 Ibid., p. 192.

13 John Middleton and David Tait (eds.), *Tribes Without Rulers*, 1958; cf. for this my 'Some Thoughts on the Relation of Political Theory to Anthropology', *American Political Science Review*, Vol. LXII, June 1968, pp. 536 ff.

14 In a chapter on legislation, chap. V of Book II, which is very brief, Godwin proclaims that 'reason is the only legislator . . . The functions of society extend, not the making, but the interpreting of law . . . It is the office of conscience to determine . . . like a British judge, who makes no new law, but faithfully declares that law which he finds already written.' (Godwin, op. cit. p. 107 citing Sterne's *Sermons*.)

15 Erik H. Erikson, *Gandhi's Truth*, 1969, observes that 'Indian culture (as have all others) made out of this special mission of saintly men a universal and often utterly corrupt institution, and Gandhi was well aware of the fact that the Mahatmaship could type him to the point of in-actuality'. And therefore 'He considered it all the more incumbent upon himself to make his spiritual power work in political realities'. And Erikson adds that 'I think the man was right who said that Gandhi, when he listened to his inner voice, heard the clamor of the people'.

16 In Daniel Guerin's selections, *Ni Dieu ni Maître—Anthologie de l'Anarchisme*, Paris 1970, we find 'La Société ou Fraternité internationale révolutionnaire' (1865), pp. 175–6.

17 H.-E. Kaminsky, *Michel Bakounine—La Vie d'une Révolutionnaire*, 1938, pp. 29–30.

18 Kaminsky, op. cit. p. 56. Proudhon did not go so far; yet in his essay on the principle of authority, selected by Guerin, op. cit., pp. 85 ff. (from Proudhon's *Idée générale de la Révolution au XIXe siècle*), Proudhon concludes: 'Concluons sans crainte que la formule révolutionnaire ne peut plus être ni législation directe, ni gouvernement direct, ni gouvernement simplifié; elle est: plus de gouvernement. Ni monarchie, ni aristocratie, ni même démocratie . . . Point d'autorité, point de gouvernement, même populaire: la révolution est là.' In Guerin, op. cit. p. 90.

19 Guerin, op. cit. p. 164

20 Ibid.

21 From Bakunin's *God and the State*, to be found in Guerin's op. cit. pp. 165–6, discussed by Woodcock, op. cit. chap. 6.

22 Ibid. (Bakunin).

23 The literature on this conflict is very extensive. The most thorough, though biased, contemporary account is that by James Guillaume, a selection from which is in Guerin, op. cit. I, pp. 142 ff. In it is reference to the slanderous story that Bakunin was an agent of the Tsarist secret police, a slander in which Marx became involved. The studies of anarchism cited in note I above all deal with it.

24 Engel's little-known essay on authority is reprinted in Wolfgang Dressen, *Antiautoritäres Lager und Anarchismus*, 1968, which contains other selections from anarchist writings. Engel's essay is at pp. 110 ff. It is found in Karl Marx/Friedrich Engels, *Werke*, Berlin 1962, Vol. 18, pp. 305 ff.

25 This pamphlet of Lenin's is of 1902; though a *pièce de circonstance*, it has assumed a central place in later years. Comments on it are found in most writings on Soviet Communism for which see Alfred Meyer, *Leninism*, 1957, chaps. II and VI.

26 Kropotkin, *Mutual Aid*, 1902, *passim*.

27 For the 1961 party program see Herbert Ritvo (ed.), *The New Soviet Society*, 1962 (published by *The New Leader*).

28 Bakunin in Guerin, op. cit. p. 159; the passage is found in the pamphlet 'La Commune de Paris et la Notion de l'Etat', 1870.

29 The Spanish anarchists are treated in Joll, op. cit. chap. IX, and esp. Kraemer-Badoni, op. cit. pp. 262 ff. From the Spanish anarchists' own viewpoint, Augustin Souchy, *Anarcho-Syndikalisten über Bürgerkrieg und Revolution in Spanien*, 1969, seems most informative.

10/Tradition and Authority Vindicated

1 The notes for this chapter will be restricted to a few which are needed for additional reference; for the rest, they are contained in those cited for the preceding chapters of the work.

2 Oscar and Mary Handlin, *The Popular Sources of Political Authority*, 1966.

3 Samuel P. Huntington and Clement H. Moore (eds.), *Authoritarian Politics in Modern Societies—The Dynamics of Established One-Party Systems*, 1970.

4 Ibid., p. 44.

5 Thomas Hobbes, *Leviathan*, chap. 16.

6 Ibid., chap. 26.

7 Ibid., chap. 26.

8 Edmund Burke, *Works*, Vol. IX; cited in *The Philosophy of Edmund Burke, A Selection*, Louis I. Bredvold and Ralph G. Ross eds., 1960, p. 18. Cf. also the brief discussion in Francis P. Canavan, *The Political Reason of Edmund Burke*, 1969, pp. 126–7.

9 But that never meant for Burke that the people should exercise it. 'The people are the natural control on authority; but to exercise and to control together is contradictory and impossible.' (*Works*, Vol. III, 416). What he meant by such a statement he made clear in his 'Address to the King': 'We have too early instructed and too long habituated to believe, that the only firm seat of all authority is in the minds, affections, and interests of the people, to change our opinions on the theoretic reasonings of speculative men, or for the convenience of a mere temporary arrangement of state.' (*Works*, Vol. V, 135.)

10 Thomas D. Wheldon, *The Vocabulary of Politics*, 1953, pp. 50–56, offers such a conclusion.

11 Joseph de Maistre, *Du Pape*, new edn, 1843, chaps. II and III, the latter entitled 'Définition et autorité des Conciles'.

Bibliography

It goes without saying that authority constitutes a topic in most of the great classics of political theory. It did not seem worthwhile to list these, except for a few of special importance. Volume I of the annual *Nomos*, 1958, was entirely devoted to authority. Some individual papers are listed below.

ACTON, LORD, *Essays on Freedom and Power by John Emerich Edward Dalberg-Acton* (ed. Gertrude Himmelfarb), Beacon Press, Boston 1948.

ALMOND, GABRIEL, *The American People and Foreign Policy*, Harcourt, Brace, New York 1950.

ALMOND, GABRIEL A. and COLEMAN, JAMES S., *The Politics of Developing Areas*, Princeton University Press, Princeton, N.J. 1960.

ALMOND, GABRIEL A. and VERBA, SIDNEY, *The Civil Culture: Political Attitudes and Democracy in Five Nations*, Princeton University Press, Princeton, N.J. 1963.

ARENDT, HANNAH, 'What is Authority?', in *Nomos*, I, *Authority*, Harvard University Press, Cambridge, Mass. 1958.

BAKUNIN, M., 'La Commune de Paris et la Notion d'Etat', in *Oeuvres*, 6 vols., Paris 1896–1914.

—— *God and the State*, Dover Publications, New York 1970.

BANFIELD, EDWARD C., *Political Influence*, Free Press, Glencoe, Ill. 1961.

BEYME, KLAUS VON, *Die Politische Elite in der Bundersepublik Deutschland*, Piper Verlag, Munich 1971.

BRUCK, E. F., *Über römisches Recht im Rahmen der Kulturgeschichte*, Springer Verlag, Berlin 1954.

CANAVAN, FRANCIS P., *The Political Reason of Edmund Burke*, Duke University Press, Durham, N.C. 1960.

DAHL, ROBERT A., *Who Governs? Democracy and Power in an American City*, Yale University Press, New Haven 1961.

DE GRAZIA, SEBASTIAN, 'What Authority is Not', *American Political Science Review*, Vol. 53, 1959.

DICEY, A. V., *Introduction to the Study of the Law of the Constitution*, Macmillan & Co., London 1886.

DICKINSON, JOHN, 'Social Order and Political Authority', *American Political Science Review*, Vol. XXIII, 1929, pp. 293–328, 593–632.

DRESSEN, WOLFGANG (ed.), *Antiautoritäres Lager und Anarchismus*, Wagenback, Berlin 1968. Contains Engels' brief essay on authority.

DURKHEIM, EMILE, *Le Suicide*, 2nd edn, Presses Universitaires de France, Paris 1960, summarized in Sebastian de Grazia, *The Political Community*, University of Chicago Press, Chicago 1948.

ERIKSON, ERIK H., *Gandhi's Truth—On the Origins of Militant Nonviolence*, Norton, New York 1969.

FAIRBANK, JOHN K. (ed.), *Chinese Thought and Institutions*, University of Chicago Press, Chicago 1957.

FRIEDRICH, CARL J., *Man and His Government*, McGraw-Hill, New York 1963. Esp. chaps. 4, 12, and 33.

—— *Constitutional Government and Democracy: Theory and Practice in Europe and America*, 4th rev. edn, Blaisdell Publishing Co., Boston 1968.

—— *The Philosophy of Law in Historical Perspective*, 2nd edn, University of Chicago Press, Chicago 1963.

—— *The New Belief in the Common Man*, Little, Brown & Co., Boston 1942.

—— *Transcendent Justice*, published for the Lilly Endowment Research Program in Christianity and Politics by the Duke University Press, Durham, N.C. 1964.

—— 'Political Leadership and the Problem of Charismatic Power', *Journal of Politics*, Vol. 23, 1961.

—— 'Some Thoughts on the Relation of Political Theory to Anthropology', *American Political Science Review*, Vol. LXII, June 1968.

—— 'Authority, Reason, and Discretion', in *Nomos*, I, *Authority* (Friedrich ed.), Harvard University Press, Cambridge, Mass. 1958.

FRIEDRICH, CARL J. and BRZEZINSKI, Z. K., *Totalitarian Dictatorship and Autocracy*, Harvard University Press, Cambridge, Mass. 1956. Revised second edition 1965.

GREENSTEIN, FRED I., 'The Benevolent Leader: Children's Images of Political Authority', *American Political Science Review*, Vol. 54, 1960.

GUÉRIN, DANIEL (ed.), *Ni Dieu ni Maître—Anthologie de l'Anarchisme*, F. Maspero, Paris 1970.

HANDLIN, OSCAR and MARY (eds.), *The Popular Sources of Political Authority*, Belknap Press of Harvard University Press, Cambridge, Mass. 1966.

HARNACK, ADOLF, *Lehrbuch der Dogmengeschichte*, J. C. B. Mohr, Freiburg i.B. 1888–90. An English translation is found under the title *History of Dogma*, Russell & Russell, New York 1958.

HEDEMANN, J. W., *Die Flucht in die Generalklauseln*, J. C. B. Mohr, Tuebingen 1933.

HEINZE, R., 'Auctoritas' in *Hermes*, Vol. IX, 1925.

HESS, ROBERT D., 'The Socialization of Attitudes Toward Political Authority: Some Cross-National Comparisons', *International Social Science Journal*, Vol. 15, 1963.

HIPPEL, FRITZ VON, *Die Perversion von Rechtsordnungen*, J. C. B. Mohr, Tübingen 1955.

HUBERT, RENÉ, 'Le Principe de l'Autorité dans l'Organisation Démocratique', Paris 1926.

JACOBSON, NORMAN, 'Knowledge, Tradition, and Authority: A Note on the American Experience', in *Nomos*, I, *Authority*, Harvard University Press, Cambridge, Mass. 1958.

JASPERS, KARL and ROSSMANN, KURT, *Die Idee der Universität*, Springer-Verlag, Berlin 1946. English translation, Karl Deutsch, ed., Beacon Press, Boston 1959.

JENKS, CHRISTOPHER and RIESMAN, DAVID, *The Academic Revolution*, Doubleday, Garden City, N.Y. 1968.

JOUVENEL, BERTRAND DE, *The Pure Theory of Politics*, Cambridge University Press, Cambridge, England 1963.

KROPOTKIN, PETR A., *Mutual Aid: A Factor of Evolution*, McClure, Phillips & Co., New York 1902.

LERNER, DANIEL and LASSWELL, HAROLD D., *The Policy Sciences*, Stanford University Press, Stanford, Calif. 1951.

LINDZEY, GARDNER (ed.), *Handbook of Social Psychology*, Addison-Wesley Publ. Co., Cambridge, Mass. 1956.

LIPSET, SEYMOUR MARTIN, *The First New Nation—The United States in Histori-cal and Comparative Perspective*, Basic Books, New York 1963, esp. the con-clusion of chap. 9.

LOCKE, JOHN, *Two Treatises on Government*.

MACHIAVELLI, NICOLO, *The Discourses*.

MAISTRE, JOSEPH DE, *Du Pape*, chaps. II and III.

MIDDLETON, JOHN and TAIT, DAVID (eds.), *Tribes Without Rulers*, Routledge & Kegan Paul, London 1958.

MILLER, WALTER B., 'Two Concepts of Authority', *American Anthropologist*, New Series, Vol. 57, 1955.

MOMMSEN, THEODOR, *Römisches Staatsrecht*, Shirzel, Leipzig 1871.

NIEBUHR, REINHOLD, *The Nature and Destiny of Man: A Christian Interpreta-tion*, Nisbet & Co., London 1941.

PEABODY, ROBERT L., 'Perceptions of Organizational Authority: A Comparative Analysis', *Administrative Science Quarterly*, Vol. VI, 1962, pp. 463 ff.

PERELMAN, CHAIM and OLBRECHTS-TYTECA, L., *The New Rhetoric—A Treatise on Argumentation*, trans. by John Wilkinson and Purcell Weaver, University of Notre Dame Press, South Bend, Ind. 1969. The French original was published by Presses Universitaires de France, Paris 1958.

POLANYI, MICHAEL, *Personal Knowledge*, Chicago University Press, Chicago 1958.

—— *The Tacit Dimension*, Doubleday, Garden City, N.Y., 1966.

POUND, ROSCOE, 'Authority and the Individual Reason', *The Dudleian Lecture* at Harvard University, April 13, 1943.

PYE, LUCIAN W., *Politics, Personality, and Nation Building: Burma's Search for Identity*, Yale University Press, New Haven 1962.

RADIN, MAX, his article on tradition in the *Encyclopedia of the Social Sciences*.

ROSENAU, J. N. (ed.), *Approaches to Comparative and International Politics*, Northwestern University Press, Evanston, Ill. 1966.

ROUSSEAU, *Contrat Social*.

SCHELER, MAX, *Der Formalismus in der Ethik und die materiale Wertethik*, M. Niemeyer, Halle a.d.S. 1921.

SCHEUCH, ERWIN K. (ed.), *Die Wiedertäufer der Wohlstandsgesellschaft—Eine kritische Untersuchung der 'Neuen Linken' und ihrer Dogmen*, Markus Verlag, Cologne 1968.

SCHMITT, CARL, *Legalität und Legitimität*, Duncker & Humblot, Munich, Leipzig 1932.

SIMMEL, GEORG, *Soziologie—Untersuchungen über die Formen der Vergesell-schaftung*, 2nd edn, Duncker & Humblot, Munich 1922, chap. III (also in English in *American Journal of Sociology*, 1896–7).

SMITH, P. H. NOWELL *et al.*, 'Politics, Psychology, and Art', in Aristotelian Society, *Symposium: Science and Politics, Supplement of their Proceedings*, Vol. 33, London 1949.

SOMIT, ALBERT and TANENHAUS, JOSEPH, *American Political Science—A Profile of a Discipline*, Atherton, New York 1964.

—— *The Development of American Political Science—From Burgess to Behavioralism*, Allyn & Bacon, Boston 1967.

SPINOZA, *A Theologico-Political Treatise*.

SPIRO, HERBERT, 'Authority, Values, and Policy', in *Nomos*, I, (ed. Friedrich), *Authority* Harvard University Press, Cambridge, Mass. 1958.

SUTHERLAND, ARTHUR E., *Constitutionalism in America*, Blaisdell Publ. Co., New York 1965.

WALTZ, KENNETH N., *Foreign Policy and Democratic Politics*, Little, Brown & Co., Boston 1967.

WEIZSAECKER, CARL FRIEDRICH VON, 'Die Rolle der Tradition in der Philosophie' in *Hundert Jahre Philosophische Bibliothek, 1868–1968*, 1968, pp. 27–42.

WOODCOCK, GEORGE, *Anarchism—A History of Libertarian Ideas and Movements*, World Publishing Co., Cleveland 1962.

Select Bibliography

ARENDT, HANNAH, 'Authority in the Twentieth Century', *Review of Politics*, 1956. A challenging statement of Arendt's interesting view.

—— *Fragwürdige Traditionsbestände im politischen Denken der Gegenwart*, Europäsche Verlagsanstalt, Frankfurt a.M. 1957. The English translation is entitled *Between Past and Future—Six Exercises in Political Thought*, Viking Press, New York 1961. Stimulating and often too extravagant.

BARNARD, CHESTER I., *The Functions of the Executive*, Harvard University Press, Cambridge, Mass. 1938. Important because of its general organization theory.

BERLIN, ISAIAH, *Four Essays on Liberty*, Oxford University Press, London 1969. A discriminating statement by a friend of liberty.

BURKE, EDMUND, *Works*. The great classic on tradition.

HUNTINGTON, SAMUEL P. and MOORE, CLEMENT H. (eds.), *Authoritarian Politics in Modern Societies—The Dynamics of Established One-Party Systems*, Basic Books, New York 1970. This collection clearly describes the emergence of a new authoritarianism.

JOLL, JAMES, *The Anarchists*, Eyre & Spottiswoode, London 1964. Clearly shows the misunderstanding of authority on the part of the anarchists.

JOUVENEL, BERTRAND DE, *Sovereignty: An Inquiry into the Political Good*, Cambridge University Press, Cambridge, England 1957. One of the outstanding new theories. From the original *De la Souveraineté: A la Recherche du Bien Politique*, Génin, Paris 1955.

KARIEL, HENRY S., *In Search of Authority: Twentieth Century Political Thought*, Free Press of Glencoe, New York 1964. An interesting collection under a rather pretentious title.

LASSWELL, HAROLD D. and KAPLAN, A., *Power and Society*, Yale University Press, New Haven 1950. Authority discussed within a systematic context of political theory.

LEWIS, GEORGE C., *An Essay on the Influence of Authority in Matters of Opinion*, J. W. Parker, London 1849. Clearly recognizes the rational component of authority.

LLEWELLYN, KARL, *Jurisprudence: Realism in Theory and Practice*, University of Chicago Press, Chicago 1962. A forceful statement of the notion of precedent.

MEAD, MARGARET, *Soviet Attitudes Towards Authority: An Interdisciplinary Approach to Problems of Soviet Character*, McGraw Hill, New York 1951. A brilliant anthropologist's assessment of authority in the Soviet Union.

MICHELS, ROBERT, 'Authority', in *Encyclopedia of the Social Sciences*, Vol. II, 1930. The article is a good summary of 'conventional wisdom' on the subject.

PEABODY, ROBERT L., *Organizational Authority: Superior-Subordinate Relationships in Three Public Service Organizations*, Atherton, New York 1964. This is an interesting comparative analysis from a sociological perspective.

PERELMAN, CHAIM, *Le Champ de l'Argumentation*, Presses Universitaires de Bruxelles, Brussels 1970. Interesting for its stress on the role of authority in legal argumentation.

PROUDHON, *Idée Générale de la Révolution au XIXe Siècle*, Gernier Frères, Paris 1851. Another firm anarchist rejection of authority.

RUDOLPH, LLOYD I. and HOEBER, SUSANNE, *The Modernity of Tradition—Political Development in India*, University of Chicago Press, Chicago 1967. Though focused on a specific case, contains important general insights.

STIRNER, MAX, *Der Einzige und sein Eigentum*, O. Wigand, Leipzig 1845. The English translation is entitled *The Ego and His Own*, B. R. Tucker, New York 1907. Probably the most extreme anti-authoritarian statement.

WEBER, MAX, *Wirtschaft und Gesellschaft*, 2nd edn, J. C. B. Mohr, Tuebingen 1925, chap. I. An English translation is found in *Max Weber: The Theory of Social and Economic Organization*, trans. by A. M. Henderson and Talcott Parsons, Free Press, Glencoe, Ill. 1947. A very influential analysis from the sociological perspective, but misleading.

WELDON, THOMAS D., *The Vocabulary of Politics*, Penguin Books, Harmondsworth, England 1953. Sets out boldly, but arrives only at a confused traditional notion.

YELAJA, SHANKAR A., *Authority and Social Work—Concept and Use*, University of Toronto Press, Toronto 1971. A valuable collection of extracts and papers to illustrate the universal role of authority in all kinds of organizations.

Index